WORLD WAR II
MASSACHUSETTS

WORLD WAR II
MASSACHUSETTS

···

James L. Parr

THE
History
PRESS

Published by The History Press
Charleston, SC
www.historypress.com

First published 2024

Manufactured in the United States

ISBN 9781467156431

Library of Congress Control Number: 2023949609

CONTENTS

Above: The Agnew family, 1945. My mother is seated in the second row, far left. *Author's collection.*

Left: My father, PFC George Parr, in Assam, India, 1945. *Author's collection.*

This book is dedicated to my parents, Kathleen Agnew Parr and George Donald Parr. Both grew up in the Mattapan section of Boston and both served their country during the war. My father, Don, enlisted at age eighteen in 1943 and, after induction at Fort Devens and training at Fort Dix, served as an army private assigned to the 102nd Chemical Processing Company in China, Burma and India (CBI). My mother, Kaddy, graduated from High Park High in 1944 and at the age of sixteen worked at the Boston Army Base in the message decoding department. The wartime experience of the Agnews was like that of many other families across the state. My mother's older brother Ed was in the navy and brother Gerald was in the army. Both her father and sister Jeanne worked at the navy yard, and even the two youngest boys, Jimmy and Paul, were frequently dressed in sailor suits. All three of my father's older brothers were stationed overseas with the military; they all returned safely. Both of my parents had fascinating wartime stories, some of which they shared over the years. I wish I had asked them for more.

APPRECIATION

My sincere thanks to the many people who assisted me in the writing of this book:

Bob Cullum for permission to use the amazing photos from the Leslie Jones Collection

Lynne Damianos for scanning images

Kara Fossey of the Fort Devens Museum for making research materials available

Mike Kinsella at The History Press for assisting in every step in the development of this book

Johanna McBrien and Nicole McAllister at the Dedham Museum and Archive for leading me to some interesting stories

Jay O'Brien for sharing photos and stories of his grandparents' dog, Bessie

Kevin O'Donnell for sharing information about his father, Walter, and Raymond Hickey

Kevin Swope for proofreading

Ruthann Tomassini and the Framingham History Center for helping me locate the grave of Raymond Hickey

Eric Wiberg for providing information and images related to U-boat activity and the sinking of the *Lark*

Special thanks to my sister Kathy Dimare for starting me on my World War II journey of discovery when she gave me *The American Heritage Picture History of World War II* on Christmas Day 1971.

Chapter 1

PREPARATION

In 1940, there were 4,316,000 people living in Massachusetts, with 770,000 of them residing in the city of Boston. Those citizens got their news from the eight daily Boston papers and four local radio stations in operation at the time. Beginning with the invasion of Poland on September 1, 1939, readers and listeners closely followed the events in Europe, hoping that the United States would not be dragged into the conflict but feeling that it was inevitable. In a Gallup poll conducted in 1939, almost half of those surveyed believed the United States would end up in the European war.

Great Britain and France had both declared war against Germany two days after the invasion of Poland, but it wasn't until the summer of 1940 that Brits experienced the full consequences of that action. Beginning in July and intensifying in September, the German Luftwaffe regularly bombed England's largest cities in what was to become known as the Blitz. The reports and images coming from the destroyed cities moved many to support military aid to the beleaguered nation, but isolationists were concerned about being pulled into the European conflict if such aid were given. On March 11, the same day that the U.S. Army passed the one-million-soldier mark, President Roosevelt signed the British aid bill known as Lend-Lease, authorizing the transfer of American-produced food, equipment and weapons to Britain and other allied countries, with the expectation that the material would be returned (unlikely) unless it was destroyed (highly likely).

Massachusetts Democratic senator David I. Walsh echoed the sentiments of many of his constituents when he stated, "One need not look during the debate about providing weapons and equipment to beleaguered Britain. I say it is too risky, too dangerous, to try to determine how far we can go, tapping the resources of our own Government and furnishing naval vessels, airplanes, powder, and bombs. It is trampling on dangerous ground." Whatever views one held concerning American involvement in the conflict, one did not need to look beyond the borders of their own state to see that this was indeed a country preparing for war.

1940

In April 1940, groundbreaking ceremonies were held at Westover Air Base in Chicopee. The base would welcome its first battalion in July.

The Federal Office of Civilian Defense was established in May with New York mayor Fiorella La Guardia as its head. First Lady Eleanor Roosevelt would join him a few months later, as newsreels regularly showed a devastated London following repeated German bombing raids. Towns began organizing auxiliary police and fire units and Civilian Defense committees. Drilling for these groups commenced on town commons. Individual towns organized classes for air raid wardens; in Quincy, two fourteen-year-old Camp Fire girls were the youngest applicants on record. Libraries sponsored talks by experts who advised citizens on how to combat toxic gas or put out fires caused by incendiary bombs.

The first sinking of an American freighter by a German U-boat, the *Robin Moor*, out of New York on its way to Cape Town, grabbed headlines all summer as readers anxiously awaited news of the fate of the forty-six passengers and crew. The attack was first reported by the captain of a Brazilian freighter who had picked up eleven survivors about nine hundred miles off the South American coast nineteen days after the sinking. The remaining passengers and crew were rescued a few days later, and in mid-July, many of them arrived back in the United States on a ship docking in Charlestown. Three of the crew were from Massachusetts: second officer Robert Taylor of Salisbury, able seaman Joe Johnson of Watertown and cabin steward Hugh Murphy of East Boston. After returning home, the affable Murphy related his ordeal to reporters, describing being awoken in the early morning on May 21 and seeing the U-boat a short distance away. The U-boat signaled the freighter, demanding a boat and officer with papers be sent, and the first officer of the freighter complied. Upon his return, the officer announced that the captain had given a thirty-minute deadline to grab supplies and abandon ship. "When it was all over, we all had to admit the submarine commander was darn nice about it. He just had a job to do," Murphy told the press. When the four lifeboats carrying passengers and crew were about a mile distant, the submarine crew fired one torpedo and shelled the deck of the *Robin Moor* until it sank. Officials with the cargo line denied that the freighter was carrying any weapons or other war materiel.

The etiquette of the U-boat captain notwithstanding, the sinking of the *Robin Moor* marked a turning point in U.S.-German relations and convinced many Americans that war was inevitable. It was a prelude to the U-boat action that would occur in the waters off the Bay State in the coming months.

In August, the Massachusetts Committee on Public Safety was formed at the directive of Governor Leverett Saltonstall, with 150 prominent citizens serving under executive director John Wells Farley. By the time of the Pearl Harbor attack some sixteen months later, the committee had instituted a civil defense plan that put Massachusetts at the forefront of preparedness in the event of an enemy attack.

The nation's first peacetime draft was enacted in September. All men ages twenty-one to forty-five were required to serve for one year if called. The lottery commenced on October 29 when a blindfolded Secretary of War Henry Stimson reached into a large glass container and pulled a capsule containing the first number, 158. In East Acton, twenty-seven-year-old Alden Flagg Jr. beat the odds in more ways than one when his number was pulled, making him the first draftee, just as his father, Alden Sr., had been in the World War I draft lottery. Many of the young men bearing the lucky number told reporters they were fortunate to be called and eager to do their service. Of the 250,000 required registrants in the Greater Boston area, 70,000 were estimated to be eligible with a 1-A (available for service) classification.

The following day, President Roosevelt arrived in town to deliver a campaign speech at Boston Garden. He was in a race with Republican Wendell Wilkie, a businessman who had never held political office. Voters were concerned about FDR's pursuit of a third term, which, although not prohibited by law, had never been done before. They were also worried that the president was leading the country into war in Europe. Polls that fall showed that while 60 percent of voters approved of some form of aid to Great Britain, 88 percent were against entering the war. On Election Day, November 5, Roosevelt and running mate Henry Wallace were victorious with 54.7 percent of the vote over Wilkie's 44.78 percent.

1941

The New Year saw "lucky" winners in the draft lottery across the state leaving their homes to begin their year of mandatory military service. The departure of young men from their hometowns often elicited a patriotic response from citizens that harkened back to a bygone era. In Dedham, residents gathered in the town square to bid farewell to each new wave of draftees. Accompanied by selectmen, a marching band and color guard of VFW and American Legion members, each group of draftees marched from the swearing-in ceremony at the courthouse to the railroad station. This tradition would continue for the duration of the war and present a particularly poignant scene in 1944 when Phillip Jackson, after performing the drumming duties he had so often done, turned over his drumsticks and boarded the train to Boston for induction into the army.

War bonds were introduced across the country as defense bonds in April 1941, offering an opportunity for all citizens to contribute to the war effort regardless of age or financial status. Government bonds had been used to finance military needs during the Civil War and again in World War I with limited success. The purchase of a bond was essentially a loan to the government that would be paid back with interest later. Secretary of the Treasury Henry Morgenthau adapted and improved the features of the previous two bond campaigns, offering the bonds at a fixed rate and marketing them directly to the average citizen, rather than pushing for purchases by banks and institutions. The bond program was deliberately intended to be more than a capital-raising venture; it was a strategically executed propaganda program designed to raise the consciousness of the American people and unite the citizenry in a morale-boosting war on the enemy.

To take on this task, Morgenthau appointed Peter Odegard, professor of political science at Amherst College and propaganda specialist. For the symbol of the bond program, Odegard chose a landmark that was both beloved in Massachusetts and recognized as a symbol of freedom around the world: the Concord Minute Man statue. The statue was sculpted by Daniel Chester French in 1871 and stood at the foot of the Concord Bridge, where a group of farmers and part-time soldiers had taken on the British army on that first day of the American Revolution. For the next four years, French's iconic statue would be seen on posters, billboards, newspaper ads, newsreels and every other item associated with the bond program.

On Independence Day, Massachusetts residents enjoyed their last fireworks display for five years. Although municipal fireworks displays returned after

Posters like this one featuring the Concord Minute Man statue were used to promote the sale of war bonds. *Author's collection, scan by Damianos Photography.*

the war, the manufacture and sales of all personal fireworks were outlawed permanently in the state in 1943.

In the baseball All-Star Game in Detroit on July 8, Red Sox outfielder Ted Williams hit a game-winning three-run homer in the ninth inning to lead the

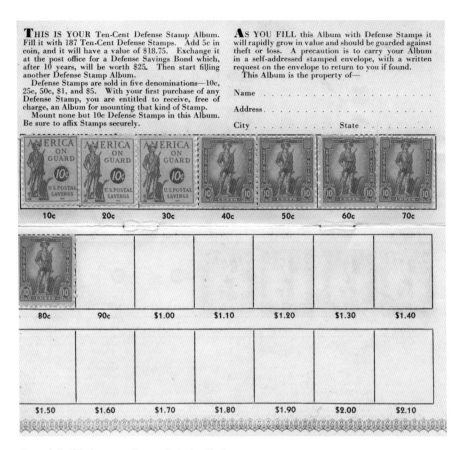

A partially filled stamp album. *Author's collection.*

American League team to a 7–5 victory over the National League. Williams had been tearing up the league all season with his hitting, finishing with a .406 batting average (which has yet to be equaled), thirty-seven home runs and 120 runs batted in. Despite the presence of four future Hall of Famers in the lineup, the Sox finished in second place, a distant seventeen games behind the Yankees.

In early August, consumers got a preview of the shortages and rationing that would become a part of their daily lives once the war began. Silk imports from Japan had been severely curtailed, and on August 2, domestic silk production was halted and all shipments from warehouses were frozen in order to save the precious material for potential wartime use. Silk stockings were a basic element of women's fashion at the time, and the announcement caused concern among millions of retailers and consumers alike. It was estimated that Boston's retail stores had about a six-month supply of stockings on hand, but women would have to get creative after that. Some women considered going bare-legged. Others switched to cotton, while still others opted for nylon stockings, which had been introduced the previous year and accounted for about one-fifth of all stocking sales. Department stores that had plentiful inventory of silk saw frenzied shoppers competing for the coveted hosiery. Gilchrist's Department Store renamed its nylon offering "Victory Stockings" and in an open letter to customers chastised those who were hoarding the precious silk stockings and encouraged women to buy the new nylon product for only seventy-nine cents per pair. As time passed, the silk ban forced the shutdown of hosiery mills across the country, including the Fitchburg Weaving Company.

A second blow to residents of the state came that same week when tight restrictions were imposed on the sale of gasoline. Beginning Monday, August 3, nighttime gasoline sales were banned; all gas stations across the state had to close from 7:00 p.m. to 7:00 a.m. Long lines formed on that

Women in Boston show their patriotism by going bare-legged. *National Archives and Records Administration (NARA).*

Sunday as motorists filled up one last time before the curfew went into effect. Thousands of drivers who were unaware of the new rule found themselves stranded on the side of the road with empty gas tanks.

As residents dealt with the silk shortage and gasoline ban, the White House announced that President Roosevelt would be taking a short vacation on the presidential yacht USS *Potomac*. Accompanying the president and the crew on the ten-day "fishing trip" somewhere off the New England coast were his personal physician, Rear Admiral Ross McIntire, Major General E.M. Watson and the president's canine companion, Fala. After taking a special train from Washington, the group arrived at the navy submarine base in New London, Connecticut, and boarded the 150-foot yacht. No press members were allowed on the boat, and a news blackout was imposed for the duration of the journey. The White House assured the public that the president would be following war news on the radio and promised regular updates throughout the trip.

A dispatch from the *Potomac* a few days later described both the weather and the fishing as good, and the presidential party tanned and enjoying the cool ocean breezes after a humid Washington summer. Several Cape Cod residents reported seeing the presidential yacht leisurely heading up the canal with FDR himself on deck, trademark cigarette and holder in his mouth. Except it wasn't him, but rather a Secret Service agent impersonating the president, who was hundreds of miles away on the deck of a different vessel, amid a secret conference with the prime minister of Great Britain, Winston Churchill.

Despite the presidential staff's attempts at subterfuge, rumors had been swirling for several days that such a meeting was taking place somewhere off the coast of Canada in the North Atlantic. Details of the trip and the conference would be revealed weeks later after FDR had safely returned to Washington via Rockland, Maine.

After spending just a few days in Buzzards Bay, the *Potomac* rendezvoused with the USS *Augusta* off the coast of Martha's Vineyard, where FDR and his staff boarded the ship and headed for the Newfoundland coast. Churchill, in the meantime, was cruising toward the rendezvous aboard the HMS *Prince of Wales*. On August 9, the two leaders met for the first time as heads of their respective governments.

The result of the meeting was a document known as the Atlantic Charter, announced on August 14 after Roosevelt had arrived back at the White House. In the declaration, Roosevelt and Churchill laid out plans for a postwar Europe with eight principles describing how the people and

The presidential yacht *Potomac* in the Cape Cod Canal, 1938. *NARA.*

governments of the occupied countries would be restored to a peaceful existence. The charter was not a formal agreement or treaty, and despite Churchill's urgings, the president offered no promises of U.S. intervention in the war. Most importantly, the meeting was the beginning of a friendship between the two leaders that would become more significant after the United States entered the war just a few months later.

On September 23, a crowd of 100,000 gathered at the Fore River Shipyard in Quincy to watch the launch of the newest battleship to be built, the thirty-five-thousand-ton USS *Massachusetts*. The 750-foot-long battleship slid down the ways after being christened with the traditional champagne bottle by Mrs. Charles Francis Adams, wife of the former secretary of the navy under Herbert Hoover.

The army's air defense command announced in November the formation of a volunteer air warning program, and towns began training volunteers and setting up air watch stations on the tallest buildings and highest hills. "Plane spotters" across the state would be keeping a vigilant watch over the skies of Massachusetts for the next few years.

The newspaper headlines in the days leading up to the attack on Pearl Harbor primarily concerned events in Europe, in particular the U-boat threat in the North Atlantic. Reports of tensions between the American and

Japanese governments were routinely found on page four or five. Only in the last weeks leading up to the attack did war seem likely; experts predicted that an attack could occur in the Philippines or some other nearby island. On Friday, December 5, readers learned that Japanese diplomats were looking to extend talks "in the hope of finding some formula to make the Pacific more peaceful."

Chapter 2

REACTION/ADAPTATION

On December 7, 1941, the Japanese attack on Pearl Harbor made the Pacific much less peaceful than diplomats had promised just a few days earlier. Responses varied, but the general mood was one of shock and anger. In Fall River, textile workers showed their patriotism by canceling a proposed strike and pledging to stay on the job. Former Boston mayor James Michael Curley showed his anger by returning an honorary medal that had been awarded him by the Japanese government in 1917. Fear of another attack was realistic and shared by government leaders and ordinary citizens alike. The events of Tuesday, December 9, illustrate the overriding fear that gripped the state, but they also highlight the determination, sense of cooperation and level of preparedness that would define the country, and Massachusetts in particular, in the difficult years ahead. For ninety minutes on that day, residents in the Boston area and other Northeast coastal cities believed that the country was once again under air attack from enemy planes. An air raid siren at 12:45 p.m. sent jittery residents running into the streets, frantically listening for radio announcements and looking to air raid wardens for direction.

Naval yard workers and suburban schoolchildren were sent home, off-duty firemen and medical personnel reported for duty at their stations and traffic was stopped from entering Boston. Governor Saltonstall came on the radio to confirm that the warning was not a drill and enemy planes were only two hours away. Despite the distressing announcement and the anticipated death and destruction of such an attack, most Boston citizens remained calm and followed defense procedures and precautions for which they had been training for the better part of a year.

After a tense few hours, officials determined that there was no actual threat of attack, and the all-clear signal was given at around 2:30 p.m. Further investigation revealed that the source of the misinformation was the air base at Marshall Field, New York, where radio operators mistakenly believed that Washington had sent an official warning of an attack.

Military and government officials found a silver lining in the aftermath of the scare. The false alarm had given defense organizations a chance to rehearse in the event of a genuine emergency, and those organizations had performed admirably without panicking. Communication breakdowns and flaws in the warning system were noted, and meetings were scheduled to discuss ways to improve the response. Governor Saltonstall returned to the airwaves that evening, stating, "Events of the past two days have proved with alarming clarity that distance of our attackers does not limit the range of their assaults. We must be prepared to meet them anywhere within the limits of our nation for the protection of our men, women, and children and for the preservation of the principles of life which we uphold."

The events of that week did not prevent the city from continuing the tradition of lighting the trees at Christmastime on Boston Common. "If they're going to bomb Boston,'" one official remarked, "let 'em bomb the Common."

CIVIL DEFENSE

Massachusetts had been preparing for war for at least eighteen months prior to the Pearl Harbor attack, beginning in August 1941 with the formation of the Massachusetts Committee on Public Safety. That committee developed a civil defense blueprint for each of the state's 351 cities and towns. Many local groups had already begun their work prior to December 7. Almost half a million volunteers served at the local level under the guidance and direction of the state committee. Residents were trained as air raid wardens, blackout wardens, medical staff and auxiliary police officers and firefighters. Until the operation and its volunteers were placed on an "as-needed" status in June 1944, the civil defense program, after the military, was the state's most important protection against enemy invasion.

BLACKOUTS, DIMOUTS AND AIR RAID DRILLS

One thing that all of us can and should do is to prepare our homes against possible enemy air raids. This is important not only for our own protection but for the safety of the whole area in which we live. Not every town is an important target, but every lighted community may be a beacon that guides enemy planes to their targets.
—What Can I Do: The Citizen's Handbook for War

The threat of an enemy air attack was real and persistent, especially in coastal towns and cities. Civil defense officials did all that they could to enforce the rules and regulations designed to make potential targets less obvious to the enemy. The shining golden dome of the Massachusetts State House was seen as especially inviting, and so in March 1942, two coats of battleship gray were applied to the Beacon Hill landmark.

Skyglow is the illumination of the night sky from artificial sources. This light made cities much more visible and helped silhouette ships at sea, making them easy targets for U-boats. To prevent skyglow, coastal cities and

A worker paints the dome of the Massachusetts State House in March 1942. *Courtesy of the Boston Public Library, Leslie Jones Collection.*

A local model reminds citizens to follow dimout regulations, 1943. *Courtesy of the Boston Public Library, Leslie Jones Collection.*

towns instituted both blackouts and dimouts. During a blackout, the goal was to achieve total darkness in homes and businesses for a short period, until a perceived enemy threat was over. In June, a regional blackout was practiced to determine the amount of skyglow of the coastal towns. Civil defense committees would hold occasional blackouts at the local level to gauge their community's readiness in the event of an actual air raid. For most of the war, towns on the East Coast operated under dimout conditions. Dimout rules for Massachusetts were tightened after voluntary participation fell short of expectations. The Massachusetts Committee on Public Safety published the following dimout regulations in November 1942: "All lights shall be permanently shielded, obscured, or reduced in intensity so that no gleam or reflection therefrom shall be visible from any point on the seacoast north of Old Saybrook, Connecticut inclusive. If they cannot be so shielded or controlled, they shall be extinguished."

The outer edge of the dimout area was a north–south line that ran from Lowell through Framingham into Rhode Island, about twenty-six miles from the coast. Streetlights used lower-wattage bulbs and were reduced in number. Automobile headlights were blacked out on top, and cars in coastal towns had to park facing away from shore. The nighttime speed limit was reduced to thirty miles per hour. Outdoor Christmas light displays were prohibited. The dimout was in effect from one hour before sunset until one hour after sunrise, and the hours of the dimout were published daily in newspapers to remind citizens and help them avoid fines or arrest. In Boston, an air raid siren was sounded to indicate the start of the dimout hours.

"ENEMY" ALIENS

Germany and Italy declared war on the United States on Thursday, December 11, two days after President Roosevelt had classified Germans, Italians and Japanese living in the country as "enemy aliens." This status severely limited the movement and privileges of all unnaturalized citizens from those countries. Approximately 200,000 enemy aliens in the state were required to turn in firearms, short-wave radios and cameras to the nearest police station by January 5, 1942. All would need to register their status and be fingerprinted by the end of February. Any travel outside their town had to be approved a week in advance. While there were few Japanese people living in the state and small populations of Germans in some cities and towns, this ruling mostly affected the large Italian population living in Boston, Pittsfield and other locations. The large Italian fishing fleet out of Boston was immediately grounded by the captain of the port, who feared that fishermen might convey diesel fuel and other supplies to enemy submarines, even though many of those affected had lived in Boston for decades and had sons in the service.

Thousands of people reported to their local post offices to register by the February 28 deadline, while FBI surveillance resulted in several raids, particularly in neighborhoods close to defense plants. Confiscated items were stored at the Springfield Armory for the duration. After persistent lobbying from Italian American organizations, enemy alien status was lifted for Italians only in November 1942. Germans and Japanese would retain that status for the duration.

For the next four years, residents would experience changes in their daily lives that would range from subtle to significant. The themes of life on the homefront were adaptation, conservation, confusion and frustration.

RATIONING

Conservation is a war weapon in the hands of every man, woman and child. And here are two simple rules for using your weapon:
1. Get along with less.
2. Take good care of the things you have
—The Citizen's Handbook for War

Residents in the Northeast had already had a taste of rationing when silk distribution was halted and gas sales were restricted the previous summer. Now that the nation was at war, precious metals and other resources were reserved for military production, and common consumer goods became scarce or unavailable altogether. Restrictions were placed on the purchase of a variety of items, from shoes to typewriters. Domestic automobile production ended on January 1.

The new year also saw the rationing of rubber, as supply lines from Malaya and the Dutch East Indies were cut off. This had the biggest consumer impact on the tire industry, but rubber was an essential material used in the manufacture of many other products, including gloves, boots,

These taxis in Boston lost their tires to the scrap drive. *Courtesy of the Boston Public Library, Leslie Jones Collection.*

girdles, garden hoses and toys. The rubber shortage even changed the game of baseball when, in 1943, a redesigned "balata" baseball was used in place of the traditional rubber-centered ball. Balata comes from a tropical tree of the same name and had no essential wartime use, nor did it have the same bounce as rubber. Souvenir balls hit into the stands became harder to come by, due not only to the less lively baseball but also because of an unwritten rule that urged fans to turn over any foul ball or homer hit into the stands for use by troops at camps around the globe. Ballparks, including Fenway, had specially decorated collection baskets where the balls could be deposited during the game. The heated rivalry between the Red Sox and Yankees even spilled over to this charitable gesture; sportswriters noted that while New York had sent 120 dozen baseballs to service camps compared to Boston's 80 dozen, it was because of Yankee Stadium's larger dimensions.

Gasoline sales that had already been reduced were now rationed on the East Coast in May, and drivers were encouraged to use public transportation, walk, "double up" or avoid unnecessary travel altogether. The use of bicycles was promoted until bicycle sales were suspended in April, and permits were issued in July for workers in certain categories. The city of Quincy, despite its four hundred workers at the shipyard, was issued a mere forty permits; similarly, Lynn received only thirty-five. Smaller towns got as few as two permits, but soon, bikes appeared throughout the cities and towns of the Bay State. Boston mayor Maurice Tobin and his wife vowed to use pedal power throughout his term in office.

HITCH OLD DOBBIN TO THE SHAY AGAIN

Retailers dependent on trucking for local transportation were not only affected by the tire rationing but were also concerned about the difficulty in obtaining truck parts for repair. As a result, workhorses returned to the streets of many cities and towns after an absence of twenty years or more. While the resurgence of horse-drawn buggies, carriages and shays may have brought back nostalgic memories of a bygone era, it also created new problems for public works departments. Although horse-drawn wagons delivering ice or milk were still found on the streets of a few towns, most communities had not seen equine traffic since the 1920s, and in the intervening years, significant changes had been made to roadways, traffic patterns and regulations.

The city of Springfield had to refer to an ordinance from 1902 to issue its first hackney license in over twenty years. Street surfaces proved to be too smooth and slippery for iron horseshoes, especially in wet weather, but rubber horseshoes were not available. Amenities for horses such as watering troughs had been either removed, converted to planters or filled with cement. At one time, Boston had dozens of watering troughs throughout the city, but health officials had shut them down in the 1920s after they were found to be spreading equine diseases. Most were disconnected from the city water supply, removed and put in storage, but some of the more decorative ones remained in place. In Newton Centre, an elaborate stone fountain dating from 1880 was repaired and rededicated by Mayor Goddard and MSPCA president Dr. Francis H. Rowley on June 26, 1943.

Within six months of Pearl Harbor, the equine business was making a comeback. The stable business in Boston tripled. Commercial businesses utilized horses for deliveries of items such as milk, groceries and newspapers. The Model Dairy in Pittsfield made retail deliveries exclusively by horse and special-ordered two wagons from Illinois to round out its fleet. The Boston Post Office issued a request for wagons and horses to deliver Christmas

This watering trough, which was reactivated in World War II, still stands in Newton Centre. *Photo by author.*

Horses made a comeback in cities: a horse-drawn sightseeing tour in Boston. *Courtesy of the Boston Public Library, Leslie Jones Collection.*

packages in 1942. *Boston Herald* delivery trucks had been loaned to the Red Cross for war use, and so its entire fleet was converted to horse-drawn wagons. An enterprising tour company in Boston named itself Victory Sightseeing tours and offered horse-drawn tours of the city, as well as excursions to the old Wayside Inn in Sudbury.

The resurgence of the horse was not confined to the Bay State but was a national movement. A reworking of the 1909 song "Put on Your Old Gray Bonnet," called "Hitch Old Dobbin to the Shay Again," commented on the use of the horse in place of cars. It was sung on the *Fibber McGee and Molly* radio show in January 1943 and again on the *Edgar Bergen and Charlie McCarthy* show in March.

This comeback of workhorses was not without its problems. As more horses were put to work, oats and other forms of feed became scarce, and the novelty began to wear out. Comedian Jack Benny commented on a quite different wartime use for horses in this exchange with announcer Don Wilson from the February 1943 broadcast of his popular radio show:

> *Jack: Don, speaking of horses, I wouldn't be surprised if all track records were broken this year. Racehorses will run faster than ever before.*
> *Don: How do you know?*
> *Jack: They've got to; it's either that or the meat market. Imagine losing two dollars on a nag and a week later paying twenty-four cents a pound for him.*

The lions in the Franklin Park Zoo were the first to get a taste of this new menu offering when it was announced in July 1942 that their everyday diet of beef would now consist of horse meat. It was only a few months later that government agencies were promoting horse meat for human consumption.

The government offered several compelling arguments for the addition of horse meat to the family dinnertime menu: it was nutritious, readily available and could be purchased without ration points. Horse meat was common fare in Europe, especially France. In September, the Supreme Market in Quincy advertised ground horse meat at twelve and a half cents a pound. In December, an executive for the Clinton Beef company reported selling thirty thousand pounds of the meat in three days, prompting this *Herald* headline: "Bostonians Hitch Old Dobbin to the Frying Pan." The W.H. Smith Company of North Street offered various horse steak cuts at thirty-five cents per pound (beef steak was selling at eighty-nine cents per pound), roasts at twenty-five cents and frozen meat at eighteen cents. "Horse

Meat Is Tender and Tasty," a *Globe* ad proclaimed. "Europeans have been eating it for years...in fact by choice. So will you...when you learn how much like beef it really tastes." The faculty club at Harvard was getting fifteen to twenty orders per day for their luncheon special featuring a horse meat steak, onions and potato salad.

Anticipating the possible shenanigans of passing off horse meat as beef, the Boston health commissioner passed regulations forbidding the use of horse meat as hamburger or sausage and requiring the lettering on packages to be at least one inch high. Eventually, the government established a horse meat ceiling price of twenty cents per pound, but as the war dragged on, shortages and black-market prices helped curtail the demand.

Meat was but one of many food items to be in short supply or rationed for the duration. The federal Office of Price Administration (OPA) was a wartime agency that determined which commodities would be rationed. Local volunteer boards helped distribute ration books. Coffee was rationed from November 1942 until July 1943. In January 1943, a government ban on sliced bread was instituted to conserve steel used in the manufacture of bread slicers. Pre-sliced bread had been available since 1928, and the ban prompted Bond brand and Life brand breads to run newspaper ads instructing consumers in the fine art of bread slicing. The ban was widely criticized by consumers and even caused near-riots in the few retail stores that managed to offer sliced bread for sale. When the ban was lifted just a few short months later in March, Wonder Bread ran a full-page *Globe* ad that perfectly captured the nation's relief over the return of this convenience: "What a joy to not have to slice bread! What a blessing that children may once again help themselves to good bread! Now, more than ever before in these days of food rationing and shortages, Wonder Bread comes as a godsend!"

To facilitate the registering of families for sugar ration cards in May 1942, the government turned to a group that was skilled in crowd management and organization: teachers. From May 4 to 8, to the joy of students, classes across the Commonwealth were canceled and registration centers were set up at schools. Over five million users were registered by the volunteer teacher staff in just four days. In Middlesex County, ration cards were stored at the state police barracks in Framingham and delivered to cities and towns under police escort. A week later, the teachers were called upon once again to register families for gas rationing.

Banned in Boston

Induction centers across the state were flooded with enlistees, and soon the sight of uniformed soldiers and sailors was common, especially in port cities like Boston. The growing numbers of service members across the country prompted First Lady Eleanor Roosevelt to caution young women against marrying their beaus in haste before they were sent overseas. "A hasty marriage does not always turn out well even though you enter it because of patriotic fervor," she warned in her weekly radio broadcast. Those in uniform enjoyed a certain level of esteem in the community, but for those who did not serve, it was quite a different story.

Lew Ayres was a well-known movie actor who had gained his greatest popularity playing a war-scarred soldier in the 1930 drama *All Quiet on the Western Front*. He later starred in the Dr. Kildare serial for MGM, playing the earnest and hardworking title character in eight films beginning in 1938. In April 1942, *Dr. Kildare's Victory*, the ninth title in the series, was playing in theaters across the state. But by the end of the month, the film had been withdrawn from movie houses from coast to coast, and the mention of Lew Ayres's name elicited strong feelings from theatergoers and non-movie fans alike. At issue was the actor's military classification as a conscientious objector (CO).

While Ayres was not a member of any organized religion, he had long been a deeply religious man and had developed his own personal spirituality through his studies of philosophy and spiritualism, as well as his reading of the Bible and the works of Ralph Waldo Emerson and Carl Jung. Ayres had been a Red Cross first aid instructor and practicing vegetarian for years and had made public statements calling killing "the worst sin," affirming that he could never take a human life. When war broke out, Ayres was willing to serve in the medical corps, where he could put his Red Cross training to use. Neither the army nor his close Hollywood circle ever doubted the sincerity of his convictions, and though they did not agree with his position, many defended his right to follow his conscience. Some Massachusetts citizens had a different opinion, however.

The Empire Theater in New Bedford was one of the first movie houses to withdraw the Kildare picture after the local American Legion Post objected. They replaced the feature with *Joe Smith, American*. Theaters in Pittsfield, Ayer and North Adams soon followed. On April 7, the Boston City Council passed an ordinance requesting the city censor revoke the license of any theater that showed a Lew Ayres picture.

The actor did have his local supporters. The *Harvard Crimson*, in an editorial titled "Objection Overruled," opined, "This sort of hysterical condemnation is like refusing to teach German or boycotting Wagnerian opera."

"To attack Ayres' right to obey his own conscience is worse than absurd, it's dangerous," wrote Reverend Orlando Tibbetts of the Trenton Street Baptist Church in a letter to the editor of the *Globe*. "Why do people call this a 'war for freedom' when the freedom of conscience is denied all men? Has the thing that our forefathers died for been scrapped for narrow-minded bigots who refuse to see that even in war the conscience works in some people?"

As with all conscientious objectors, Ayres was sent to a camp in Oregon, where he spent several months working alongside about one hundred other COs performing forestry work. Eventually, the army allowed the actor to serve as a noncombatant medic, and after training in Texas, Ayres was sent to the Pacific, where he was one of the first servicemen to land during intense

Corporal Lew Ayres (*in helmet*) on Leyte Island, October 1944. *NARA.*

fighting in Leyte and Luzon. There he served as a chaplain's assistant and won three battle stars. He donated all his army pay to the Red Cross. Ayers's service satisfied theater operators, who had no objection to promoting his next film, *Fingers at the Window*, which opened in Boston on June 25. Ayres continued a successful movie and TV career after his wartime service and was nominated for an Academy Award for his performance in *Johnny Belinda* in 1948. He died in 1996 at the age of eighty-eight.

It did not take long for the citizens of Massachusetts to adopt a wartime routine and to accept as ordinary those circumstances that only months before would have been unthinkable. For thousands, joining the service gave them a sense of purpose and a feeling of usefulness in the fight. For those who were unable to serve in the military, there were dozens of volunteer organizations performing vital work on the homefront.

Chapter 3

PARTICIPATION

Enlistments in the army and navy increased dramatically in the week following the Pearl Harbor attack. Draft-aged men formed long lines at recruitment centers to show their patriotism and to land a military assignment of their choosing. Banks and post offices saw their biggest sales days for defense bonds. As the weeks passed, increased opportunities arose for Bay Staters to find a way to contribute.

New employment opportunities opened as commercial manufacturing converted to the production of military goods. Bond drives and salvage drives fostered good-natured competition between groups, while creating an air of excitement with the frequent appearances of Hollywood's most glamorous stars. The Defense Department even found a way for the family pet to do its part!

BOND DRIVES AND FUNDRAISERS

Shortly after the start of the war, the Defense Bond program became known as the War Bond program, and all citizens, even the very young, were encouraged to do their part. Bonds could be purchased through employee programs, at banks and at bond rallies. The federal government held eight bond drives, a period of about four to six weeks when bonds would be heavily promoted with advertising, signs, radio programs and events. Quotas were

Opposite, top: Hundreds of volunteers enlisted during the navy's "Lexington Volunteers" recruitment drive in 1942. *Courtesy of the Boston Public Library, Leslie Jones Collection.*

Opposite, bottom: The Suffolk War Bond Center opened on Bromfield Street in Boston in 1942. *Courtesy of the Boston Public Library, Leslie Jones Collection.*

Above: Interior of Suffolk War Bond Center with promotional posters. *Courtesy of the Boston Public Library, Leslie Jones Collection.*

Right: A war bond stamp album. Note the word "war" is stamped over the word "defense." *Author's collection.*

set by employers and town governments, and the progress toward these goals was charted on wall posters or published in town weeklies. With each new bond drive, the government would create a marketing campaign featuring a slogan. Bond rallies as well as fundraisers for service organizations were often held at large venues with entertainment by popular recording artists and movie actors.

HOLLYWOOD COMES TO BOSTON

On May 1, 1942, a star-studded spectacle known as the Hollywood Caravan arrived in Boston for an Army-Navy Relief Fundraiser after crossing the country. Included in the caravan were such box office stars as Cary Grant, Laurel and Hardy, James Cagney, Groucho Marx, Bob Hope and Hope's sidekick, Boston native Jerry Colonna. A crowd of twenty-five thousand welcomed the stars after their arrival by special train at South Station. At one point, Groucho Marx left the train and walked the length of the

Military Police escort three Hollywood stars at South Station on May 1, 1942. *Left to right:* Boston native Jerry Colonna, singer Risë Stevens and radio comedian Bob Hope. *Courtesy of the Boston Public Library, Leslie Jones Collection.*

platform into South Station, where he bought a tube of toothpaste. When he tried to get back on the train, military personnel did not recognize him without his iconic greasepaint mustache and would not let him board until he produced identification.

Later, under an escort of soldiers from Camp Edwards, the performers boarded open-backed cars and greeted the thousands of fans lining the streets along the route from the Hotel Statler to Boston Garden. At the Garden, the troupe performed musical numbers and comedy sketches featuring Olivia de Havilland, Charles Boyer and Cowardly Lion Bert Lahr. The finale of the event was a performance of "Yankee Doodle Dandy" by James Cagney, accompanied by a chorus line of eight dancing Hollywood starlets. Over $75,000 was raised from ticket sales and the auctioning of autographed programs.

Sixth War Loan Drive

In November 1944, husband-and-wife comedy team George Burns and Gracie Allen arrived in Boston to perform their live radio show and kick off the Sixth War Loan Drive at a benefit at Boston Garden. The couple had been performing together as a comedy team since their vaudeville days, and their popular radio show had been on the air for over twelve years. Upon their arrival at South Station, Gracie was made honorary mayor for the day, after which she promptly raised salaries, lowered taxes and gave city employees the day off.

The couple performed their regular Tuesday night live broadcast of their radio show at Symphony Hall. The plot of the story centered on Gracie's attempts to get George a singing appearance at the upcoming benefit, appealing to both Arthur Fiedler and Governor Saltonstall for help. (A running gag on the show was George's inflated opinion of his less-than-melodious singing voice.) At one point, Gracie declared that George's appearance would make Boston as famous as Worcester! The performance received a rousing response from the audience of employees of Lever Brothers of Cambridge, manufacturers of Swan soap, the show's sponsor.

The following night. George and Gracie were the featured performers at a rally for the Greater Boston United War Fund held at Boston Garden. An audience of 13,500 was treated to a show that included Arthur Fiedler and the Boston Pops, the military band from Camp Myles Standish and a male

George Burns and Gracie Allen entertain a crowd at the Boston Garden in November 1944. *Courtesy of the Boston Public Library, Richard Merrill Collection.*

chorus of shipyard workers from the Fore River shipyard in Quincy. The highlight of the evening was Gracie's performance of the comic "Concerto for Index Finger," during which a frenzied Fiedler and the orchestra tried to keep up with the musical hijinks of the daffy comedian.

"Incendiary Bums"

The hanging or burning of effigies of hated public figures is a centuries-old form of protest that experienced a nationwide revival once the war began. Of the three Axis leaders, Mussolini, Hirohito and Hitler, the German dictator was by far the most despised figure to be torched. The burning was often the main attraction at bond rallies and scrap drives, sometimes preceded by a "Parade of Horribles," another old New England tradition featuring bands, costumed marchers and, of course, a barrage of insults and curses hurled at the stuffed mannequins by onlookers.

A secret group of Harvard students called the "Crimson Cult" got a head start on the fad in February 1941 when they hanged and burned Hitler on the banks of the Charles River, nearly igniting the leader of their group in the process. A garage owner in Brighton hanged the Fuhrer in honor of five of his employees who were in the service. A large rally at Great Barrington in January featured the wailing of fire engines, a rider dressed as Paul Revere delivering letters addressed to soldiers and the burning of effigies of the three "incendiary bums" on the steps of town hall. In Milton, a stuffed Hitler hung at the entrance to the town's scrap heap. At a rally on Boston Common sponsored by radio station WEEI, children and adults alike were encouraged to "drive a nail in Hitler's coffin" by purchasing war bonds.

The odyssey of one effigy created for a bond rally in Natick illustrates both the creativity and the strong emotions of Massachusetts citizens during this time. The rally began on August 31, 1942, with a Horribles Parade that ended at the town common. The parade included marching bands and a hay wagon bearing the hanging effigies of Mussolini, Hitler and Hirohito. A Lou Gehrig autographed baseball fetched $1,000 at an auction hosted by Red Sox manager Joe Cronin and radio personalities Judy Canova and Jackie Cooper.

The finale of the evening was the midnight burial of Adolf Schicklgruber (a mocking name often given to Hitler under the mistaken belief that it was his actual last name). The wooden coffin containing the effigy was planted under the grass on the common at the stroke of midnight as the band played the jazz tune "I'll Be Glad When You're Dead, You Rascal You."

Several days later, the effigy was disinterred by patriotic townsfolk who did not want it spoiling their town common and unceremoniously left at the Waltham dump. From there, the coffin was taken to Boston Common by a group of movie executives who auctioned it off to the first person to purchase a $500 war bond. In a nod to the rebels who pulled off the Boston

Above: Burning or hanging the German dictator was a popular attraction at salvage drives and bond sales. *Courtesy of the Boston Public Library, Leslie Jones Collection.*

Left: Wearing their Sunday best, a group of girls lets Hitler have it on Boston Common in August 1942. *Courtesy of the Boston Public Library, Richard Merrill Collection.*

Opposite: The Japanese "suicide sub" arrived in Boston in May 1943. *Courtesy of the Boston Public Library, Leslie Jones Collection.*

Tea Party, the winner of the auction, Lena Becker of Chelsea, attempted to dump the coffin in Boston Harbor at T Wharf but was stopped by Coast Guard officials. Undeterred, Becker and her accomplices dragged the coffin to the Summer Street bridge and tossed it into Fort Point Channel, where it was eventually washed out to sea.

A JAPANESE SUB

In the spring of 1943, the Treasury Department sponsored a nationwide tour featuring a captured Japanese "suicide sub." The seventy-eight-foot, forty-ton midget submarine was one of five launched by the Japanese during the attack on Pearl Harbor. While the other four subs sank to the bottom of the sea along with their two-man crews, one sub washed up on the beach at Oahu, and its lone surviving crew member became the first POW of the war.

The cross-country tour began in October 1942 in San Francisco and arrived in Boston on May 21, 1943. Military bands greeted the special

A patriotic jubilee on the Charles River Esplanade in May 1942, before dimout regulations were tightened. *Courtesy of the Boston Public Library, Leslie Jones Collection.*

trailer carrying the sub and escorted it to its staging area on Tremont Street adjacent to the Common. Free tickets were distributed to anyone purchasing war bonds or stamps. Viewers mounted a specially constructed platform and looked through thirty plexiglass portholes that had been installed by the navy after the sub's capture. Inside were replica torpedoes and even uniformed wax crew members at the controls. After its successful Boston appearance, the sub moved on to Worcester, Fitchburg, Holyoke, Pittsfield and then New Hampshire and Vermont.

On May 24, 1942, a Victory pageant was held at the Hatch Shell on the Esplanade. Twenty-two thousand people attended this patriotic jubilee that featured enlistment drives for all three branches of the service, a parade of citizens from various nations and a large lighted "V for Victory" stairway with uniformed sailors waving from the stairs.

SALVAGE DRIVES

Many communities had already begun planning and enacting salvage drives when Governor Saltonstall announced the "Victory through Salvage" campaign on January 10, 1942. Over the next few months, cities and towns mobilized their residents and businesses to "clean their attic" for scrap iron, steel, paper, rags and rubber. To motivate citizens, it was announced that the Atlantic Avenue Elevated tracks (El), in disuse for several years, would be dismantled and the estimated ten thousand tons of steel would be available for the manufacture of 570 light tanks or thirty-two thousand bombs. The Massachusetts Committee on Public Safety announced it would seek out abandoned bridges and streetcar rails for salvage. The committee also spread the word to fishermen to be on the lookout for discarded rubber tires, bedsprings and other useful materials they might snag while angling.

There was no end of items that could be salvaged and recycled. When the Jordan Marsh store appealed to customers to turn in old silk and nylon stockings to be used for smokeless powder bags for the army, they received over thirty-five thousand pairs. Bandleader and local celebrity Vaughn Monroe led a drive to collect 300,000 old records in order to reclaim the shellac they contained after shellac from India was cut off.

In February, newly appointed director of salvage Garth F. Chambers stated his support for a plan to salvage the hundreds of captured World War I German tanks and cannons on display at town halls, commons and VFW posts throughout the Commonwealth. The enthusiastic response from communities went far beyond the original suggestion, as armament dating back to America's earliest conflicts soon found its way to the scrap heap. The roundup of aging weaponry was an opportunity for cities and towns to display their commitment to victory and stir the patriotic spirit. The

Children were some of the most enthusiastic scrappers. *Courtesy of the Boston Public Library, Leslie Jones Collection.*

Brookline American Legion Post donated its World War I tank to the drive in an elaborate ceremony, the tank bearing a sign reading, "We're turning this in for a 1942 model." The Pittsfield Legion replicated the journey of Revolutionary general Henry Knox, conveying its historic cannon along the trail taken by Knox in 1775 to bring cannons to General George Washington in Boston. The cannon was auctioned for $375 to a scrap dealer on Boston Common, along with a cannon from the USS *Constitution* donated by Everett Legionnaires that netted $50. The town of Dedham also sacrificed its cannon from Old Ironsides, scrawling the message "To the Axis from Dedham" on the side.

When the supply of ancient artillery across the state was exhausted, eager salvagers found another source of readily available metal. Decorative iron railings, fences and gates dating from the nineteenth century were found in abundance across the state in cemeteries and on the grounds of public buildings, and soon these found their way to the scrap heap.

Governor Saltonstall got the ball rolling on October 5 when he exited the Massachusetts State House wearing a crisp dark suit and tie, goggles and welder's gloves. In the shadow of the gray painted dome and in front of a crowd of onlookers and press, the governor wielded a flaming acetylene torch and proceeded to obliterate the face of Adolf Hitler inscribed on a metal plaque that was attached to the iron railing that curved in front of the State House steps. Then workers dismantled the 116-year-old fence and added it to the growing scrap pile.

Not to be outdone, one week later, Boston mayor Maurice Tobin took the torch to the frilled fence surrounding City Hall on Milk Street, burning his shoes in the process. The total haul of the two fences netted fifty tons of scrap iron to be sold to dealers, who would in turn sell the scrap to the government for production of war materials.

The Town of Concord opened Junk Rally Week in November 1942 with a parade through town featuring the requisite Schicklgruber effigy. A total of 125 tons of scrap metal was collected and added to the several tons of farm machinery already donated. The iron railing around the famed Minute Man statue was promised to the drive, as was the decorative iron fencing at the

Governor Saltonstall takes a blowtorch to the Fuhrer, commencing the removal of the State House's decorative iron fence, October 1942. *Courtesy of the Boston Public Library, Leslie Jones Collection.*

PUBLIC LIBRARY, CONCORD, MASS.

An early twentieth-century postcard showing the ornate fence that once stood in front of the Concord Free Public Library. *Author's collection.*

town's library. The Concord Free Public Library still stands on Main Street, and a close inspection of the granite blocks that border the scenic lawn reveals a series of holes that once held the iron fence posts. Fifty miles away, the North Adams library was stripped of all the decorative iron adorning the inside and outside, including railings, lighting fixtures and fireplace pieces. Eighty-year-old Charlotte Bragg of Marblehead offered the century-old fence surrounding her family's cemetery plot, stating, "I know if my father and mother and other dear ones who are buried there were alive, they would want me to do just what I am doing."

While some of the fences were eventually replaced (including at the State House and old City Hall), a visit to local libraries and graveyards will often reveal the telltale holes where iron was removed—reminders of how citizens sacrificed their past to ensure victory in the present.

Recently, historians have questioned the impact of the millions of tons of scrap metal, paper, rubber and other materials collected during the war. Much of the rubber collected had already been recycled once and was not suitable for new products. Only virgin aluminum could be used in military aircraft production, so none of the millions of pots and pans collected across the state were turned into fighter planes. Metal recycling had been a thriving

Holes like this one in Concord usually indicate an iron fence or railing was removed, most likely during a World War II scrap drive. *Photo by author.*

business for years before the war began, and while it is true that the amount of scrap metal contributed by citizens was not much more than the average amount collected annually in prewar years, the salvage drives came at an early point in the war when the nation's citizens were still feeling stunned, a bit helpless and in desperate need of a morale boost. To that end, the scrap drives were an unqualified success.

VICTORY GARDENS

In January 1942, the Office of Civilian Defense announced the Victory Garden program; such a program had first been instituted successfully during the First World War. Citizens were encouraged to plant community gardens where both the labor and the produce would be shared by families, while large-scale farming operations would be reserved for supplying troops. Gardeners were also encouraged to can and preserve their fruits and vegetables, with some federal money available for the purchase of fertilizer, seed, jars and pressure cookers.

Boston mayor Maurice Tobin at the opening of the Victory Garden on the Common, April 1943. *Courtesy of the Boston Public Library, Leslie Jones Collection.*

Locally, gardens were planted on town greens and college campuses and in backyards. In April 1943, Mayor Tobin dedicated a Victory Garden on the Boston Common in anticipation of upcoming food shortages. The site would serve as a demonstration garden with an information booth open all day staffed by experts to help answer questions. The mayor hoped that ten thousand Boston residents would plant Victory Gardens either in their own backyards or on plots provided by the city.

"We must accept rationing whether we like it or not, and do all in our power to help ourselves and our fellowmen to meet the situation in a realistic way," the mayor remarked before breaking ground at the controls of a rototiller.

Several large garden plots were made available to residents, including locations at Franklin Park, Copley Square and the Fenway section. The Fenway Victory Gardens are still in operation some eighty years after they were first planted.

Ground Observer Corps and Civil Air Patrol

In January 1942, the civilian plane spotting program that had been announced the previous November got underway, and by December, there were some ten thousand volunteers manning over six hundred observation posts across New England. The program was organized as part of the U.S. Army Air Force's Ground Observer Corps, and in Massachusetts, it was overseen by the American Legion. At its height, about one and a half million civilian plane spotters were manning fourteen thousand observation posts in states on both the Pacific and Atlantic coasts. Plane spotters in London had been credited with thwarting German bombers on several occasions, and the hope was that American volunteers could do the same service, especially in the industrialized Northeast.

Training included identification of both enemy and friendly aircraft. Government-printed handbooks contained both silhouettes and photographs of American, British, German and Japanese aircraft. Rubber models were also provided, and youth organizations such as the Boy Scouts made plastic models to be used by the volunteers in their town. At the Jordan Marsh store, decks of "spotter" playing cards with the faces of each suit showing enemy planes could be purchased for just $1.15.

While on duty, spotters would first identify any planes flying overhead and then call the information to an army filter center, where a course of action would be determined. The observation stations were manned twenty-four hours a day, with spotters usually signing up for four-hour shifts. Volunteers included members of the Boy Scouts and American Legion, veterans from the Great War and homemakers. With their reputation for keen eyesight, major-league ballplayers made excellent observers, and in the summer of 1942, players from both the Boston Braves and the Red Sox volunteered as spotters. Braves infielder Lew Gremp was the first to sign up, and in a short time, he recruited seven of his teammates. The crosstown rivalry extended to wartime service as Red Sox manager Joe Cronin led a crew of nine players who joined the corps as well. It was the consensus of the group that future Hall of Famer Cronin was the best spotter from the Red Sox and rookie pitcher Jimmy Wallace the best of the Braves.

The government handbook for plane spotters stated, "The duties of the ground observer are often inconvenient, sometimes physically uncomfortable, almost never glamorous. No man or woman should volunteer for services looking for an easy job or with the intention of making anything other than an all-out effort to perform his or her duties efficiently and on schedule."

A page from the Identification Booklet used by the U.S. Army Air Force Ground Observer Corps. *Author's collection.*

Some towns located their watch stations on the roofs of town halls; others built observation towers on isolated hills. Most of the accommodations were simple wooden structures that were cold in winter, stifling in summer, isolated and uncomfortable. (In Williamstown, so many volunteers were suffering from colds and flu that Williams College professor Howard Stabler and his physics students developed the first-in-the-state electronic aircraft listening device in May 1942.) The hours from 2:00 to 4:00 a.m. were known as the "dog watch." Most spotters found boredom to be the most difficult aspect of the job and took up knitting, card playing or doodling to pass the time. A spotter's log kept by the Plainfield volunteer group shows the level of boredom and the creative ways by which spotters filled the long hours. Alongside the routine entries detailing time and date, weather conditions and plane sightings are pages of drawings, poems, limericks and jokes.

Plane spotting was often tedious but could also be hazardous. Forty-seven-year-old Weyman Crocker fell from a tower after his watch in Fitchburg and died from a fractured skull. Fifteen-year-old Lawrence Oucard of Milton was knocked unconscious when lightning struck the observation tower he was in at Milton Academy during a storm in July 1943.

With so many airfields located in the area, training flights by novice flyers were common, and inevitably, so were crashes. Over one hundred military personnel were killed in aircraft crashes in the state during the war years. While most of the crashes occurred at busy military airfields, many planes went down while flying over forests, farmland and crowded urban areas. Some of these crashes were witnessed and first reported by plane spotters. In June 1943, Mrs. Edward Bullard and Mrs. George Burnett were on duty in Westborough when they witnessed two P-47 Thunderbolts collide and descend to earth. One of the planes crashed onto the Boston and Albany tracks, where a train carrying seventy-five passengers was traveling from Worcester to Boston. The train was unable to stop in time and derailed on the Southborough/Westborough line. Miraculously, no one on the train was seriously injured. The second plane landed in a swampy area of Hopkinton. That pilot was able to parachute to safety; the other pilot was killed in the crash.

In several instances, witnesses describe the bravery of the pilot in maneuvering his damaged plane away from crowded neighborhoods to avoid killing people on the ground. Such was the case in 1944, when Ensign Robert McLaughlin, while on a routine flight over his hometown of Haverhill, rolled his F4U-1D Corsair, spinning out of control, crashing in a clearing and exploding on impact. Horrified witnesses to the crash included his parents, who were watching the flight from their home. A memorial plaque honoring McLaughlin's selfless act of steering the plane away from a residential area was placed at the crash site in September 2023, seventy-nine years after the incident.

The worst military crash in Massachusetts occurred in 1942, when an army troop transport with nineteen paratroopers and crew aboard crashed into the side of Garnet Peak in the western Massachusetts town of Peru, killing all but three. The Garnet Mountain Memorial marks the spot where the crash occurred in heavy fog on the night of August 15. In 1943, with the threat of air attack greatly reduced and the effectiveness of radar improved, the Ground Observer Corps program ended.

All civilian flying within fifty miles of the coast was banned for the duration, apart from a group of flyers who formed the Civil Air Patrol (CAP). Massachusetts had about three thousand licensed pilots at the time the war broke out, and over one thousand joined the Civil Air Patrol, many of them women. Using their own planes, these licensed pilots patrolled an area off the coast from Portsmouth to Block Island, on the alert for U-boat activity. The CAP was also instrumental in search-and-rescue efforts when ships were attacked by U-boats. An auxiliary unit of juniors and seniors in high school was formed in early 1943.

In August 1943, a "dead" U.S. Army Air pilot was enlisted to help recruit new volunteers for the program. Captain Arthur Stavely of Milton and West Roxbury was part of a crew flying over the North Atlantic when their A-20 light bomber crashed near shore. Stavely was the only member of the crew injured and was taken to a nearby hospital, which was not equipped for long-distance communication. When relatives in New York were informed he had crashed but was recovering, the message was mixed up, and it was believed he had died in the crash. It took nearly a month for Captain Stavely to return to his base and get word to his grieving friends and family that he was alive and well. The Civil Air Patrol still operates today as the civilian auxiliary wing of the United States Air Force.

BOSTON BOMBED

In June 1944, just one week after the D-day invasion, 160,000 bombs rained down on Boston and dozens of neighboring towns. Witnesses to the "invasion" did not run screaming from the enemy, however, but raced each other to grab the paper "bombs" of diverse colors dropped by planes piloted by members of the Civil Air Patrol. One enthusiastic lad even swam to the middle of the Charles River to retrieve one, in hopes of winning the promised prize of a war bond for his efforts.

The attack on sixteen Greater Boston towns was part of an air raid drill that had been rescheduled from the previous fall due to severe weather. Twenty planes took part, led by Major Arthur J. Tully Jr., state director of aeronautics. Lieutenant Ida Smart of Fitchburg piloted one of the planes, and women were included in the drill as part of the "bombing crew." The CAP planes took off from East Boston to drop the colored bombs: red representing incendiaries; blue, high explosives; yellow, gas bombs; and green, unexploded.

Citizens had been instructed to leave the bombs where they landed and inform air wardens of the color, quantity and location of any that they found. But many eager souvenir hunters kept the brightly colored bombs, including two that fell on the steps of the State House, one that fell in Mayor Tobin's Victory Garden and several that landed on Alumni Field at Boston College in the middle of a marching band competition. Included in the payload of the bombs were thirty thousand flyers promoting the fifth war bond drive, which had recently gotten underway. After the all-clear, Boy Scouts eagerly snatched up any unclaimed flyers to be turned in for the chance at winning a twenty-five-dollar war bond. The drill was not the smooth operation the CAP had been hoping for. The area of the bombing was reduced from fifty-nine to forty-three towns due to severe weather, and only about one-quarter of the eighty-two planes scheduled to participate got off the ground. Many commuters were stranded in subway cars on the elevated tracks for over an hour until the all-clear was given. In East Boston, Steven Balchuck and his bride-to-be, Ruth Ward, were stopped by an air raid warden on their way to the church, and guests had to wait for half an hour for the couple to arrive. This was to be the last regional air raid test of the war.

Massachusetts Women's Defense Corps (MWDC)

This organization was founded in May 1941 and was active until 1946; volunteers assisted in all phases of homefront defense, including transportation, communications, medical services, member support and air raid supervision. The MWDC was organized in military style, complete with battalions, companies, ranks and official uniforms. The group was active even before the war's start, anticipating the need for organized volunteer efforts in case of enemy invasion. In September 1941, 150 uniformed members, including Governor Saltonstall's daughter Emily, staged a mock evacuation of Boston, traveling in a caravan on back roads from the capital to Gardiner and back. After the war's start, volunteers would travel to Camp Edwards and Fort Devens for training days in all aspects of civil defense.

They published a regular newsletter and frequently hosted speaking events on a variety of war-related topics. Over eighteen thousand women served in the MWDC before it was disbanded in 1946.

KIDS LEND A HAND

Boys and girls like everybody else will have to sort themselves out and find the places where they can be most useful on the home front. You will find work at home, at school, in your Scout troop, 4-H Club, through your church or some other community organization.
—The Citizen's Handbook for War

The children of Massachusetts found many opportunities to contribute to the war effort. Their boundless energy and natural competitive spirit suited them well for scrap drives and war bond drives, and both programs offered

These Boston students, like many others, "bought" a jeep by purchasing war bonds. *Courtesy of the Boston Public Library, Leslie Jones Collection.*

rewards for youngsters who outdid their peers. Incentives ranged from free movie tickets to the privilege of christening a newly built ship. Three lucky local youngsters were rewarded for their efforts in scrap metal collecting when they traveled to the Todd Shipyard in South Portland, Maine, in 1943 to christen the Liberty ship *Daniel Webster*.

At the Frank A. Day Junior High in Newton, students purchased $2,000 worth of bonds and stamps in just three weeks and were able to cover the cost of two army jeeps. The jeeps were presented to the army in a ceremony at the school with the mayor and superintendent in attendance. Jeeps were also "bought" by students in South Boston, Marblehead, Athol, Lee, Holyoke, Fitchburg and many other cities and towns.

MILKWEED SAVES THE DAY

In the summer of 1944, children across the state were given a unique opportunity to help soldiers and sailors in far-off war zones. In June, the state Department of Public Works recommended that cities and towns refrain from removing milkweed plants along the highways and fields of the state. The War Production Board needed a million and a half pounds of milkweed pods to be used in the production of life preservers. Ordinarily,

Milkweed pods ready to be picked. *Photo by author.*

the buoyant fibers of the kapok tree found in the Dutch East Indies were used for this purpose, but the war had disrupted the supply line. The fibrous hairs of the milkweed pod, growing abundantly along roads and parking lots and considered a nuisance, were determined to be a suitable substitute. Navy testing had determined that several pounds of the floss could keep an average-sized man afloat for forty hours. The harvest began in earnest in mid-September, when the pods had matured, and by early October, under the supervision of Scouting organizations and 4-H clubs, youngsters across the state had gathered several thousand bushels. Children collected the pods in onion bags and were paid twenty cents a bag, about eight hundred pods. Two bags would provide enough pods to make one "Mae West"–type life preserver. In some towns, local organizations such as the Rotary Club sponsored competitions, awarding war bonds and other prizes to the child who collected the most pods. The milkweed pod campaign was an overwhelming success; in an unprecedented collaboration between government, industry and the youth of the nation, over two million bags were collected in thirty-one states and Canada.

Dogs for Defense

The numerous programs and organizations that emerged during the war gave every family member an opportunity to do their part—from moms saving grease and forgoing nylons, dads serving as civil defense volunteers and kids collecting milkweed pods and scrap paper. In January 1942, a new program was introduced that would allow even Fido and Rover to contribute.

The Dogs for Defense program was the brainchild of Harry I. Caesar, a New York businessman and president of the American Kennel Club. Noting that dogs, with their superior senses of hearing, vision and scent, had long been in use by both enemy and Allied armies, Caesar outlined a program that would call for the recruitment, training and deployment of at least 125,000 of the nation's pet dogs for civilian defense and military guard duty. Regional centers would be set up for intake of the "volunteers," who would be trained by professional dog trainers before being assigned to guard duty at military bases, camps, airfields and production facilities. Some recruits would even be given dangerous assignments on the front lines.

It is inconceivable that families today would willingly put the family pet in harm's way for periods of up to two years or more with the possibility that their beloved doggo might not return at all. But in 1942, the response was overwhelming, with families and even children sending letters and photos to the program's directors vouching for their dog's ability. Initially, volunteers were required to be well-behaved purebreds between one and five years old, weighing at least fifty pounds and standing eighteen inches high. As the need increased, mixed breeds were accepted (although chows were found to be unreliable and rejected).

A kennel was established in Newton as the New England intake center, and a training school was conducted in Dedham on the old Karlstein polo grounds on the banks of the Charles River. The first class of thirty-five pooches graduated in July after eight weeks of training and was sent off to undisclosed assignments following emotional farewells with their owners.

Not all dogs were successful in the program. One year after sending their German shepherd Wolf to be trained, the Frederick Corbett family of Brighton welcomed him back along with a letter from the War Dog Reception Center in Nebraska that read, "We regret to inform you that your dog Wolf…has been returned to us from seven months active duty with the armed forces of the United States because he was too friendly and not aggressive enough for war duty." Coincidentally, the mail delivery that day included Corbett's induction letter instructing him to report for army service at the end of the month.

Six-year-old English setter Mose of Milton was also returned by the army due to his friendly nature. Fourth-grader Lloyd Beckett Jr. happily greeted the dog after removing the blue star service flag that had hung in the window during Mose's absence.

One Massachusetts dog not only achieved hero status but also became a minor celebrity across the nation. Sailor was a six-year-old German shepherd living with the MacKenzie family in Randolph when the call for volunteers came. In 1943, seven-year-old Ann and five-year-old Robert MacKenzie were listening to a radio program and heard a plea for dog volunteers. Within a short time, they were saying goodbye as Sailor departed for his undisclosed assignment. The family heard no more about Sailor until December 1944, when they received a letter from Burma written by army Captain Charles M. Fallon. Fallon's letter described Sailor's courage under fire and how his intelligence had saved American soldiers on more than one occasion. In one instance, while on patrol with his handler, Technical Sergeant Russell "Rusty" Mizner, Sailor alerted to an area behind some dense brush. Mizner dropped to the ground and fired into the brush, killing two Japanese snipers. Later that day, Sailor chased down another sniper in a rice paddy, forcing him to surrender.

Near the end of his tour of duty, Sergeant Mizner wrote to the MacKenzies asking the family if he could keep Sailor, who had saved his life more than once. Understandably, the family was reluctant to part with the pet they had raised from a pup and told Mizner as such. Local and national media picked up on the story, and soon readers across the country were offering solutions to the problem. A local man offered the MacKenzies a new Irish setter pup if Sergeant Mizner were allowed to keep Sailor, but the children desperately missed their canine friend and wanted him back. Sailor was returned to

Left: Sailor with Bob and Ann MacKenzie in Randolph before the war. *Author's collection.*

Below: Bessie on guard duty. *Courtesy of Jay O'Brien and the Dedham Museum and Archive.*

Opposite: Bessie's honorable discharge. *Courtesy of Jay O'Brien and the Dedham Museum and Archive.*

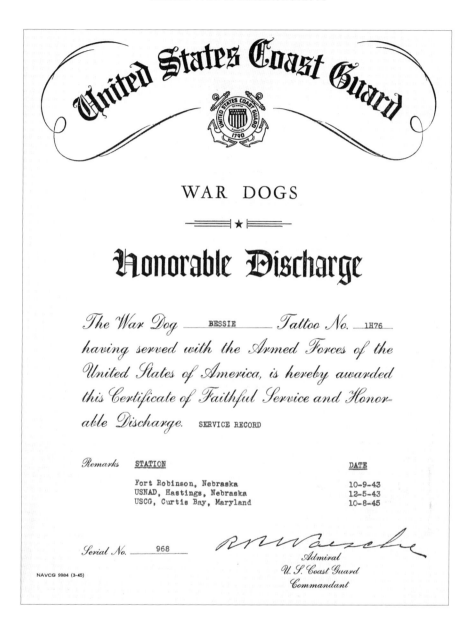

the family in March 1946. He was one of several hero dogs featured in a children's book published later that year.

Another local dog who served was Bessie, a German shepherd from Dedham, owned by Ford and Josephine Friend. When Ford Friend was unable to enlist due to his essential status as a machinist, it was decided to volunteer Bessie, who was only a few years old at the time. Bessie was assigned to a coast guard station, and coincidentally, Ford was eventually able to serve in the Coast Guard Reserve as a machinist's mate. Bessie was returned to the Fords after the war's end, displaying one behavior quirk from her time in the service: every Fourth of July when the local fireworks displays began booming and banging, Bessie would hit the ground and run for cover under the nearest table, as she had been trained. After a long, happy life with her family in Dedham, Bessie passed on and was buried in the backyard wrapped in her favorite blanket.

MANUFACTURING

Massachusetts had long been one of the country's industrial hubs, and in 1941, the state continued to be home to a thriving manufacturing center with centuries-old companies producing items for the war effort from autos to shoes to blankets. Wartime regulations and shortages forced some factories to shut down entirely, while others adapted to producing supplies and armaments for troops. The increased production and reduced workforce opened employment opportunities for women and minorities that had previously been unavailable.

The Ford Plant at Assembly Square in Somerville built over twenty thousand light armored machines known as Bren gun carriers, or universal carriers, most of which were used by the British army. The land/water carriers were designed with a low profile and mounts for six or more guns. They were manned by a four-man crew and could conquer difficult terrain. The plant won a coveted Army-Navy E Award for excellence in production in 1944. In Springfield, the Indian Motorcycle Company produced over twenty-two thousand motorcycles, most for use by forces of the British Commonwealth.

The Goodyear Tire and Rubber Company in New Bedford was a producer of life rafts and barrage balloons; these were large blimp-like balloons tethered to the ground with steel cables used as defense against air strikes.

In Leominster, the DuPont Company opened a war plant producing Lucite plastic. The plant opened three weeks ahead of schedule in April 1943, producing windshields for the noses of bombers such as the B29 Superfortress and the B32 Dominator. Initially, five hundred men and women were employed, with that number increasing as the demand for the plastic grew.

A Bren gun carrier on display at the American Heritage Museum in Hudson. *Photo by author with permission from American Heritage Museum.*

Haverhill, the shoe capital of Massachusetts, saw modifications made to the many manufacturing concerns in the city in order to produce military equipment. Factories in the city produced canteen covers, haversacks, cartridge belts, duffel bags and dozens of other items vital to a soldier's needs.

Some companies continued producing their own products, which were then shipped to soldiers and sailors serving across the globe. One such company, the New England Confectionery Company, hired additional workers in order to provide candies (including the beloved Necco wafer) to "armed forces at home and abroad."

The Boston Elevated (El) employed female conductors known as "conductorettes" for the first time in fifty years. Their duties included operating cash boxes, door controls and signals, for which they were paid sixty-five cents per hour, the same wage that men were earning.

Want ads were filled with advertisements for workers, many of them targeting women specifically, such as this Raytheon listing from the *Globe* in 1944:

About a month ago Jack went into the army. Said he didn't mind because the sooner everyone got into the FIGHT the quicker we'll have VICTORY. That started me thinking too. Now I'm a war worker at RAYTHEON and am proud of the decision I made. Not only can I save money for the day when Jack gets back, but hundreds of other girls who work here as factory trainees are "really doing something worthwhile" to help Jack and the boys WIN THAT FIGHT!

Service Flags

Service flags like these hung in windows across the state throughout the war. *Photo by author.*

Soon, windows in towns across the state were adorned with decorative service flags bearing a blue star for each member of the household serving in the military. Washington Jewelry in downtown Boston advertised the flags for eighty-nine cents each with up to three blue stars available at no extra cost. "It tells the world you've a loved one in the Armed forces of the United States," the ad read. "Thousands will be showing these flags in windows!" When a serviceman was killed, the blue star would be replaced by a gold one. In Jamaica Plain, fifty-seven-year-old widow Annie Jordan surpassed all others when she placed the tenth blue star on her service flag as her son Francis reported to Fort Devens, joining his nine brothers already serving. Businesses would often fly large service flags bearing both gold and blue stars with numbers indicating the employees who were currently in the service or had been killed.

Local Heroes

Most of the soldiers and sailors represented by these blue stars had been ordinary workers or students in civilian life; however, some who served were well known before their service or achieved recognition due to their service. All four of President Roosevelt's sons were in the service, including John, who was managing a Filene's department store in Winchester when he registered in October 1940. Fifty-year-old Boston Pops conductor Arthur Fiedler volunteered twelve hours a week as a temporary coast guard reservist in 1943. What follows are descriptions of the contributions of several Massachusetts-related individuals.

Frank Merrill

Frank Merrill was born in Hopkinton in 1903 and graduated from Amesbury High School in 1921. After six unsuccessful attempts to enter West Point (he had a vision problem), he was admitted, and after graduation, he became a career soldier. In 1942, Merrill took command of a group of soldiers who came to be known as Merrill's Marauders, a special forces unit that penetrated deep behind the Japanese lines. Merrill was appointed brigadier general in November 1943, one of the youngest soldiers to attain that rank. After American forces in Burma serving under General "Vinegar" Joe Stilwell were forced to retreat, Stilwell pledged to return and take back the country. Merrill and his marauders were instrumental in the recapture of Burma. Merrill had a heart attack in 1955 and died at the age of fifty-two. He was portrayed by Jeff Chandler in the 1962 Warner Brothers film *Merrill's Marauders*. On Veteran's Day 1999, a New Hampshire bridge on the Everett Turnpike over the Souhegan River was named "Merrill's Marauders Bridge."

Norman Cota

Brigadier General Norman "Dutch" Cota is considered by many a forgotten and underappreciated hero of World War II, and a group of historians and military enthusiasts would like to see that change. Cota's actions on Omaha Beach on D-day have been described in books and portrayed on the big screen, but he has yet to receive the widespread recognition of other military leaders of the war.

Cota was born in Chelsea in 1893 and attended Chelsea High School before transferring to the private Worcester Academy, where he earned the nickname "Dutch" while captaining the football team. His determination and hard work landed him an appointment to West Point, and after graduation in 1917, Cota returned to Chelsea for his swearing in as a second lieutenant in the army. Cota served stateside during the First World War, after which he was stationed at a number of posts throughout the country, arriving at Fort Devens early in 1941. He was appointed assistant chief of staff for the First Division and trained at Camp Edwards from August to September 1941. The day before the Pearl Harbor attack, Cota was promoted to colonel. Cota was part of invasions of both North Africa and Sicily. In early 1943, with the newly attained rank of general, Cota traveled to England, where he was named the assistant division commander of the Twenty-Ninth Infantry Division, joining in the planning of the D-day invasion.

At fifty-one, Cota was the oldest man on Omaha Beach on June 6, 1944, but throughout the battle, he showed the stamina and fearlessness of a much younger soldier, walking up and down the beach chomping on a cigar and waving his .45-caliber pistol, undeterred by the heavy gunfire and shelling from the German defenders. Cota's leadership and bravery saved countless lives that day, as he urged soldiers frozen in fear to keep moving, reportedly telling them, "You're gonna die here. Let's go inland and die." At one point, General Cota came across officers from the army's Fifth Ranger Battalion and said to them, "You Rangers got to lead the way!" In other accounts, Cota was heard shouting, "Lead the way, Rangers!" Whatever his actual words were, they were enough to spark the troops to move off the beach, and to this day, the Ranger motto is "Rangers lead the way." Throughout the battle, the general assisted the wounded, coordinated fire on German positions and motivated countless soldiers to continue the fight. General Cota's actions helped a disorganized, confused and frightened battle force overrun enemy positions and clear the beach. In July, he was awarded the Distinguished Service Cross for his courage and leadership.

Cota retired from the army in 1946 and died in 1971. He was portrayed by Robert Mitchum in the 1962 war epic *The Longest Day*. In his long and esteemed military career, he received many of the military's highest honors, including a Distinguished Service Cross, two Silver Stars and a Purple Heart. There are those who believe that General Cota should be awarded the Congressional Medal of Honor, the country's highest military award, and they continue to petition congressional leaders to take this action.

Henry Cabot Lodge Jr.

Henry Cabot Lodge Jr. may best be remembered as the Boston Brahmin Republican senator and vice-presidential running mate of Richard Nixon who was defeated by John F. Kennedy and Lyndon Johnson in the 1960 election. His army service during World War II is often overshadowed by his political career, which included terms as ambassador to South Vietnam, West Germany and the Vatican.

Lodge was first elected to the U.S. Senate as a Republican in 1936, defeating James Michael Curley. While still retaining his Senate seat, Lodge, an army reservist, was called up in April 1942 and joined forces in North Africa. As a captain in the armored division, he was among the first U.S. troops to engage German forces in combat. Lodge returned to the Senate in July after a presidential order commanded all elected representatives in the military to return to Washington or resign their positions.

The senator won reelection in November, despite criticism from Democratic opponent John Casey, who claimed that Lodge's army service had been nothing but a "Cook's tour of the Libyan desert" used to bolster his campaign. The senator stayed in Washington for a little over a year before his sense of duty and honor called him back to the military. On February 3, 1944, forty-two-year-old Lodge stunned his colleagues when he tendered his resignation from the Senate and reenlisted in the army, becoming the first senator since the Civil War to take such an action. In a letter he sent to be read on the Senate floor, Lodge wrote: "The fact that the United States is entering the period of large-scale ground fighting has, after grave thought brought me to the definite conclusion that given my age and military training I must henceforth serve my country as a combat soldier in the Army overseas. In order to serve in combat I hereby resign from the United States Senate."

Serving with the Fifth Army in Italy, Lodge put himself in harm's way while executing missions north of Rome. In September 1944, while doing reconnaissance, Major Lodge spied a German patrol some distance away. He instructed his driver to take him to their location, where Lodge captured the patrol at gunpoint and surrendered them to a nearby army unit.

Lodge's resignation resulted in a confusing game of musical chairs in Massachusetts politics over the next few years. Governor Saltonstall appointed former Newton mayor Sinclair Weeks to serve out the next ten months of Senator Lodge's term and then announced he would be running for that seat himself in a special election in the fall of 1944. That move

Senator Henry Cabot Lodge Jr. (*right*) with fellow Massachusetts senator David I. Walsh. *Author's collection.*

prompted Boston mayor Maurice Tobin to throw his hat in the ring for Saltonstall's vacant governor's seat. Both Saltonstall and Tobin won their elections, and city councilor John Kerrigan was appointed acting mayor. The shuffling continued in the fall of 1945, when former mayor and governor James Michael Curley defeated Kerrigan in the mayoral race and Lodge regained his Senate seat, defeating incumbent David I. Walsh in 1946.

Peter Saltonstall

Leverett Saltonstall, the popular Republican governor known as "Salty," first elected in 1938, was instrumental in preparing the state for the impending war. His family members also did their part in the war effort; daughter Emily was a member of the WAVES (Women Accepted for Voluntary Emergency Service), and both sons were in the armed forces, Leverett Jr. with the army and Peter with the marines. At the time of Saltonstall's reelection campaign in the fall of 1942, Peter was stationed in the Solomon Islands and had not contacted his parents for several months.

Peter was a popular pre-med student at Harvard before enlisting in his junior year. During a respite in the fighting at Guadalcanal, the young sergeant told a fellow marine and *Globe* reporter that he had enlisted because "I wanted to find out more about my fellow man and how I stacked up against them." He also remarked, "I've found my own place among my fellow men."

On August 18, 1943, the governor was in his office at the State House when the manager of the Boston Western Union office arrived to deliver in person the news that every service parent dreads—Peter had been killed in action. The next day, Saltonstall was scheduled to participate in a ceremony on the Boston Common honoring missing marine pilot Robert Hanson, who was being awarded the Congressional Medal of Honor. The governor read the remarks he had prepared before learning of his son's death and offered a personal message of sympathy without mentioning his own personal tragedy. In September, the Saltonstall family received a letter from Peter's bunkmate, PFC Benjamin Bloom, of Dorchester. In the letter, Bloom described how their squad had come under attack while patrolling on the island of Guam. Ambushed by dozens of Japanese soldiers, Saltonstall fought bravely, killing six enemy soldiers while preparing his escape. After seeing that two of his comrades were trapped by the enemy, Peter returned to the fight to allow them to escape and was killed.

Ted Williams

After the draft was reinstated in September 1940, Americans, particularly members of the press, became interested in the draft status of their favorite entertainers, actors and sports figures. In Boston, that interest centered on its star Red Sox outfielder, Ted Williams. Williams joined the Red Sox in 1939 and quickly became one of the most impactful players in the league. His batting average of .406 for the 1941 season is an achievement that no major-league player has matched. The months following the Pearl Harbor attack saw the Sox outfielder at the center of controversy concerning his draft status.

Williams had originally been classified as 3-A, deferred because he was the sole financial support for his mother. In general, Williams was supported by both hometown and rival fans, as well as servicemen who were aware of the situation with his mother. His draft status, unsurprisingly, came under scrutiny by some reporters; Williams had had a contentious relationship with the press since his first year in the league. To add to the drama and criticism, Williams was briefly reclassified 1-A (fit and available for service) in January 1942, but just as spring training was getting underway and Williams had signed a contract, his status was changed back to 3-A. Williams stated all along that he had always been willing to serve and that the deferment had not been granted at his request.

Williams was in the lineup on April 14 for the season opener against the Philadelphia Athletics, and Red Sox fans were relieved that the slugger would be with the team for the season. Then on May 23 came the surprising news that Williams had enlisted in the navy as a flight cadet. The previous day, he had secretly made his way to the Flight Selection Board on Causeway Street and been sworn in as a seaman second class. (Just three weeks later, on his eighteenth birthday, future president George Bush walked into the same office and enlisted as a seaman second class in the same program as Williams.) Three weeks previously, Williams had been approached after a game at Fenway by navy lieutenant Robert Fuller, who invited him to visit the navy base at Squantum and check out the V-5 pilot training program. A few days later, Williams and Red Sox publicist Ed Doherty drove out to Quincy, where Ted met with cadets, toured the facility and sat in the cockpit of a plane. Williams was so impressed with the program that he signed his volunteer application in the car on the way back to Fenway. That afternoon, Williams went 0-4 in a Sox 3–1 victory over Chicago.

Williams finished the season winning the American League Triple Crown (leader in average, home runs and runs batted in) with a batting average of .356 with thirty-six home runs and 137 runs batted in. The Red Sox finished a distant nine games behind the Yankees. On November 19, Williams joined rookie teammate Johnny Pesky at Amherst College to begin naval preflight instruction. Over the course of the next few years, Williams trained in North Carolina and Indiana before receiving his naval aviator wings at the naval air station in Pensacola, Florida, in May 1944.

On the morning of May 2, 1944, Williams was commissioned as a second lieutenant in the U.S. Marine Corps. Later that afternoon, he married his girlfriend of several months, Doris Soule. For the next year, Ted was a flight instructor at Pensacola. In June 1945, he arrived in Jacksonville and was on his way to Hawaii when the war ended in August.

A few weeks after his discharge in early 1946, Williams signed with the Red Sox and joined them for spring training in February. He had missed three complete seasons of baseball, and although he never saw combat, his sacrifice and service were universally praised and considered to be an

Boston Red Sox Ted Williams taking the oath for induction into the navy, May 22, 1942. *Courtesy of the Boston Public Library, Leslie Jones Collection.*

inspiration for young men across the country. In January 1952, Williams, a marine corps reservist, was called up for service in Korea and flew thirty-nine combat missions, missing almost two more seasons with the Red Sox.

Moe Berg

Another member of the Red Sox was making headlines in early 1942, but why would the retirement of a third-string Red Sox catcher and coach to join an obscure government agency be reported on the front pages of newspapers across the nation? Morris "Moe" Berg had been making headlines throughout his major-league career, but decidedly not for his accomplishments on the field. Berg achieved a lifetime batting average of .243 after spending fifteen years in the majors on three different teams, ending his playing career with the Red Sox in 1939 and then serving as a coach until his retirement in 1942. Berg's fame and popularity were owed to his wit, intellect and his achievements in various fields not typically associated with baseball.

Born in 1902 in Harlem, New York, he was often described as "the smartest man in baseball." A teammate once quipped after learning that Berg spoke seven languages, "Yeah, and he can't hit in any of them." Berg attended Princeton University, where he was a standout on the baseball team while studying seven languages, graduating cum laude in 1922. Despite his academic achievements, Berg loved baseball and signed with the Brooklyn Robins in 1923. He did continue his education, however, attending Columbia Law School during the offseason and receiving his bachelor of laws degree in 1930. In his fifteen years in the majors, "Professor" Berg was a hardworking, reliable player and a favorite with the press and could always be counted on for an entertaining interview in each city his team visited.

In January 1942, Berg accepted an assignment with the Office of the Coordinator of Inter-American Affairs (OIAA). In July, he embarked on a tour of American military bases in South America, where he made observations and recommendations for ways to improve the morale of the enlisted. But he was itching to become more involved and to do something more important, and a little more dangerous. In truth, Moe Berg wanted to be a spy.

Washington Senators first baseman Joe Kuhel chats with catcher Moe Berg in 1937. *Courtesy of the Boston Public Library, Leslie Jones Collection.*

With his aptitude for languages, his Princeton education and his ability to connect and converse with people from all levels of society, Berg was a perfect candidate for the job during the dangerous war days. And he had already had some experience working as an amateur spy. In 1934, while on a seventeen-game goodwill tour of Japan with American all-stars including Babe Ruth, Lou Gehrig and Jimmie Foxx, Berg was working for Movietone News, filming innocuous scenes of city streets, the Japanese countryside and teammates at leisure. At some point during the trip, he decided to perform a little espionage. Under the pretense of visiting the hospitalized daughter of the American ambassador, Berg donned a kimono, slicked back his hair and entered St. Luke's Hospital, one of the tallest buildings in Tokyo. Bypassing the room of the ambassador's daughter, Berg made his way to the roof and filmed scenes of Tokyo's waterfront and military facilities. Although he did not know it at the time, the footage was of little strategic value, but Berg nonetheless showed it to military officials years later. This act may have been a factor in Berg's acceptance as an agent into the Office of Strategic Services (OSS), the precursor to the CIA, in August 1943.

One of his first assignments was to travel to Italy, seek out noted physicists and determine the progress being made by the Axis on a nuclear bomb. Throughout the summer of 1944, Berg gathered intelligence on several different German military technologies. He helped recruit an Italian aeronautical engineer, Antonio Ferri, who left Italy to work in the United States on supersonic aircraft. In December 1944, the catcher pulled off a cloak-and-dagger caper that could have been lifted from the pages of a pulp magazine.

At the time of Berg's mission, the secret nuclear program known as the Manhattan Project had been progressing for three years under the guidance of Dr. Robert Oppenheimer and other top physicists. Although the team was within eight months of actual deployment of a nuclear bomb, there was still fear that the Germans would be ready first. While the Americans had Oppenheimer, the Germans had Werner Heisenberg, considered by many to be the world's best theoretical physicist. On December 12 in the city of Zurich in the neutral country of Switzerland, Berg entered a lecture hall to hear Heisenberg give a talk before a group of scientists and students. Posing as a student, Berg entered the hall concealing two deadly weapons: a pistol and a cyanide capsule. If Heisenberg gave any indication during his presentation that the Germans were close to producing a nuclear weapon, Berg was to shoot him on the spot. If necessary, he was to take the cyanide capsule to avoid capture. As it turns out, neither action was necessary. Although he had some difficulty following the mathematical and scientific points of

Heisenberg's lecture, the observant Berg noted the subdued response of the other attendees; their reaction was not what one would expect if they were just now learning that the Germans were in reach of ending the war with a nuclear weapon. The stalled status of the German nuclear program was further confirmed a few nights later by Berg as he accompanied Heisenberg to his hotel after a dinner party. During the conversation, the German physicist not only came off as being anti-Nazi but also indicated that the war was all but over for the Germans.

Berg resigned from the OSS in January 1946. He was later awarded the most prestigious American civilian honor, the Medal of Freedom, but in his own enigmatic way, he refused to accept the award. His sister donated it to the Baseball Hall of Fame in Cooperstown, New York. Moe Berg died in 1972 at the age of seventy.

Harold Russell

Harold Russell was a twenty-seven-year-old Canadian-born Cambridge resident managing a First National grocery store when Pearl Harbor was attacked. He enlisted in the army and arrived at Camp MacKall in North Carolina to train as a paratrooper with the 513th Airborne Unit. Russell was promoted to sergeant and was tasked with training new recruits in realistic battle situations. On June 6, 1944, while Allied forces were landing in France on D-day, Russell was training new recruits in mock combat with live rounds and explosives. Without warning, the explosives Russell was handling went off, injuring him severely. When he woke up in the hospital the next day, the young sergeant realized to his shock that both of his hands had been blown off at the wrists.

Russell continued his recovery at Walter Reed Hospital in Washington, D.C., where he was fitted with prosthetic hooks. In just three months, he became remarkably skillful with the hooks and returned to Cambridge, where he worked as a YMCA program director.

Russell's reputation as an optimistic and gregarious veteran so impressed army personnel that they arranged for him to be featured in a film for disabled soldiers. *Diary of a Sergeant* showed Russell going through his everyday routines adeptly using his hooks. The success of the movie prompted a war bond tour, during which Russell's affability and cheerful outlook caught the attention of Hollywood director William Wyler, who was developing a film about returning war veterans, one of whom was an amputee.

Publicity photo of Harold Russell.
Author's collection.

Wyler and Pulitzer Prize–winning screenwriter Robert Sherwood created the role of Petty Officer Homer Parrish especially for Russell in the movie *The Best Years of Our Lives*, which premiered in 1946. The film was a hit and was nominated for ten Academy Awards, including a Best Supporting Actor nomination for the Cambridge resident. At the ceremonies in Los Angeles, Russell was not expected to beat out Hollywood veterans Clifton Webb, Charles Coburn, William Demarest (who would later play Uncle Charlie on TV's *My Three Sons*) and Claude Rains (known for his work in *The Invisible Man*, *The Wolf Man* and *Casablanca*) for the award, but the Academy was so taken with his performance that they wanted to honor him in some way. Early in the ceremony, Russell was presented with a special Oscar for "bringing aid and comfort to disabled veterans through the medium of motion pictures." When Russell was announced as the winner of the Best Supporting Actor award, the crowd erupted for a full minute of applause. After making his way to the stage for the second time that night, the unassuming Russell shyly muttered, "Gosh, two Oscars is too much" into the microphone and quickly left the stage. He is the only actor to this day to receive two awards for the same role. Harold Russell resided in Massachusetts for the remainder of his life and died in January 2002 at the age of eighty-eight.

Father Joseph O'Callahan

The wartime heroism of the Kennedy brothers Joe and Jack is well documented and, in the case of John, has reached near mythical status. But they were not the only Massachusetts-born Irish Catholic heroes of the war. Cambridge native Joseph Timothy O'Callahan, a Jesuit priest, was honored by governors and the president for his bravery at sea in the waning months of the war.

"Father Joe" was born in Cambridge in 1905, attended Boston College High School and entered the Jesuits upon graduation. He received his BA from Boston College and went on to teach at BC, Weston Seminary and Holy Cross. In 1940, he enlisted as a chaplain in the navy.

On March 19, 1945, Father O'Callahan was serving aboard the aircraft carrier USS *Franklin* about fifty miles off the coast of Japan. After two intense attack waves by Japanese aircraft, the crew was catching a brief rest below decks. On deck were the carrier's planes, fuel tanks filled and laden with bombs. A lone Japanese bomber somehow evaded detection and dropped two 550-pound bombs directly on the *Franklin*. Hundreds of crew members were killed instantly, and a massive explosion and fire took place when the bombs from the carrier's planes dislodged and exploded.

Father O'Callahan had been eating breakfast when the bombs struck. He made his way to the flight deck, where he gave care to the wounded and administered last rites to the dying as ammunition and bombs continued to explode. The forty-year-old chaplain then led surviving crew members in fighting fires, tossing live bombs overboard and supervising the transfer of the wounded to the cruiser *Santa Fe*, which was skippered by Captain Harold C. Fritz of Somerville. Three more bomber attacks hit the *Franklin* before it was able to set course for Pearl Harbor, badly damaged and listing badly.

Father O'Callahan received the Medal of Honor for his bravery in a ceremony at the White House on March 23, 1946, the first military chaplain since the Civil War to be so honored. His Medal of Honor citation reads:

The President of the United States of America, in the name of Congress, takes pleasure in presenting the Medal of Honor to Commander (Chaplain) Joseph Timothy O'Callahan, United States Naval Reserve, for conspicuous gallantry and intrepidity at the risk of his life above and beyond the call of duty while serving as Chaplain on board the U.S.S. FRANKLIN when that vessel was fiercely attacked by enemy Japanese aircraft during offensive operations near Kobe, Japan, on 19 March 1945. A valiant and forceful leader, calmly braving the perilous barriers of flame and twisted metal to aid his men and his ship, Lieutenant Commander O'Callahan groped his way through smoke-filled corridors to the open flight deck and into the midst of violently exploding bombs, shells, rockets, and other armament. With the ship rocked by incessant explosions, with debris and fragments raining down and fires raging in ever-increasing fury, he ministered to the wounded and dying, comforting and encouraging men of all faiths; he organized and led firefighting crews into the blazing inferno on the flight deck; he directed the jettisoning of live ammunition and the flooding of the magazine; he manned a hose to cool hot, armed bombs rolling dangerously on the listing

Left: President Harry Truman pins the Congressional Medal of Honor on Father Joseph O'Callahan. *Author's collection.*

Below: The USS *Santa Fe* rendering assistance to the USS *Franklin* after the carrier had been hit and set afire by a Japanese dive bomber. *NARA.*

deck, continuing his efforts, despite searing, suffocating smoke which forced men to fall back gasping and imperiled others who replaced them. Serving with courage, fortitude, and deep spiritual strength, Lieutenant Commander O'Callahan inspired the gallant officers and men of the FRANKLIN to fight heroically and with profound faith in the face of almost certain death and to return their stricken ship to port.

He returned to his position as head of the Mathematics Department at Holy Cross and died in 1964. The following year, Sister Rose O'Callahan, a Dominican nun, christened the destroyer escort USS *O'Callahan*, named in honor of her brother.

Frances Sweeney

She is little known outside of a small group of present-day writers and activists who hold her in high esteem for her tireless efforts to fight bigotry in Boston both before and during the war. Frances Sweeney was a voice for tolerance when rumor and suspicion were rampant and many of the city's vulnerable citizens felt threatened, not from foreign enemies, but from their own neighbors and coworkers. Born in Brighton around 1908, Sweeney came to national prominence in October 1942 when *Life* magazine (labeling her a "fearless firebrand" and "fighting Irish girl") profiled her work for the *Boston Herald*'s "Rumor Clinic," tracking down and debunking rumors that had been plaguing the city since the start of the war.

Sweeney was the perfect choice to lead the crusade. She was already well known as an outspoken critic of antisemitism and the organizations that promoted it. A devout Catholic, she had risked ex-communication by speaking out against church leaders and public figures such as Father Coughlin, the "Radio Priest" whose controversial views were broadcast weekly.

The "Clinic" was a collaboration between the Massachusetts Committee on Public Safety, Harvard psychologist Robert Knapp and the *Herald*, which, starting in March 1942, ran a weekly column describing reader-submitted rumors that were then refuted after consultation with military officials, local law enforcement and the FBI. Rumors were also collected by a volunteer team of "morale wardens" such as bartenders, waitresses, salesmen, soldiers, sailors and factory workers. Rumors ranged from the ridiculous to the dangerous. Some believed that defense workers could not get ham because it was all being sent to Russia; others contended that the British did not bomb the Krupp manufacturing works in Germany because Winston Churchill owned stock in the company. When some women heard that the chemicals used in the perm of a female munitions worker caused her head to explode, they were fearful of going to work.

The Boston Rumor Clinic had become a national model, and soon similar operations were established in dozens of major U.S. cities by civic organizations and church and school groups. However, within days of the publication of the *Life* article, the Office of War Information (OWI) published a manual with very restrictive guidelines for the establishment of rumor clinics. The government, it seems, would rather control the narrative than an army of academics and service workers. Officials determined that the clinics actually helped spread rumors. The rumor clinics eventually faded away, and their effectiveness is still being debated to this day.

Sweeney continued her fight against injustice by starting a newspaper, the *Boston City Reporter*, and reporting on prejudice and targeted violence in both the nation and Boston neighborhoods. Sweeney recruited the city's teens to bring her tips about incidents of bullying and assaults, especially directed against the city's Jewish residents. Her investigations prompted Governor Saltonstall to form the Governor's Committee for Racial and Religious Understanding, the forerunner of the Massachusetts Commission Against Discrimination. Sadly, Sweeney's courageous crusade was cut short by a heart attack in April 1944, after a lifelong battle with rheumatic heart disease. She died two months later at the age of thirty-six.

Chapter 4

FORTIFICATION

Massachusetts has a storied military history; the "shot heard 'round the world" at Lexington marked the start of the American Revolution, and the Commonwealth had long been home to several well-established military bases, shipbuilding facilities and arms manufacturers. In the years immediately preceding World War II, additional construction added supply depots, hospitals, airfields and ammo depots, all built in an astonishingly brief period. While some of these facilities are still in operation, most were deactivated soon after the Allied victory. All had a lasting impact on the towns in which they were located. Thousands of civilians found employment, and the military personnel stationed there were welcomed as part of the community. There were costs as well; many residents were forced off land that had been in families for generations. Centuries-old dwellings were relocated or demolished, and the rural character of many communities was erased forever. The following brief descriptions of these facilities only begin to tell of their significant role in the war effort.

FORT DEVENS

Camp Devens was created in 1917 on five thousand acres encompassing the towns of Ayer, Shirley, Harvard and Lancaster as the country prepared for its entrance into the world war in Europe. In 1931, the camp became a permanent installation and was renamed Fort Devens. Devens was named

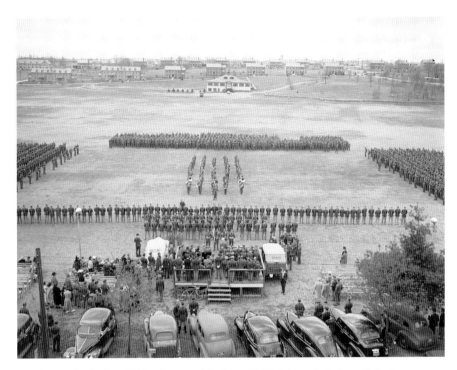

Fort Devens in the late 1930s. *Courtesy of the Boston Public Library, Leslie Jones Collection.*

the recruit reception center for the thousands of New England soldiers joining the ranks after the draft was instituted in 1940. More than 1,200 buildings were constructed to accommodate the influx of soldiers, most of whom went on to further training at other military posts. In total, over 600,000 soldiers passed through Devens during World War II.

Lovell General was built at the base in 1940 as a one-thousand-bed temporary hospital, but by war's end, it was housing over five thousand wounded soldiers. The facility also had an airfield with a 5,200-foot runway, used by both the army and navy.

CAMP EDWARDS

Camp Edwards, originally known as the Massachusetts Military Reservation, was established in Bourne as a training ground for state National Guard troops in 1936. Soon after the national draft was instituted, the state leased the camp to the army for ninety-nine years. At the time, there were only sixty-three buildings on twenty-two thousand acres, but within a few short months, construction crews had built a fully functioning camp able to accommodate thirty thousand soldiers, the largest military installation in New England. Over the next five years, thousands of soldiers were trained in a variety of military skills, including close combat, antiaircraft and amphibious warfare. The camp's coastal location provided the perfect opportunity to train troops for an amphibious assault, and the sight of hundreds of troops engaged in mock invasions was a common one on the Cape's beaches.

Crews from Camp Edwards were trained on the familiar "duck boats" at several locations. Officially labeled the DUKW, the amphibious vehicle was used throughout the Pacific islands and was a vital component of the D-day invasion. The DUKW had been in development for several years but had yet to be approved for military use when an incident off Provincetown helped to demonstrate the vehicle's usefulness. In December 1942, personnel from the Camp Edwards Engineer Amphibian Command were in Provincetown to assess the DUKW's capabilities in rough surf. On the night of December 2, crew members from the coast guard yawl *Rose*, while on routine patrol, radioed the shore command that the ship had run aground in high waves and heavy rains off Highland Light. After word reached the Amphibious

Camp Edwards in 1941. *Author's collection.*

Command at the Provincetown Towne House, a DUKW was dispatched to the beach in Truro. The craft easily made its way out to the stranded boat, and the U.S. Coast Guard crew was rescued and safely on shore in a matter of minutes. Photographer Stanley Rosenfeld was on hand to capture the rescue on film, and copies of his photos eventually made their way to Secretary of the Navy Henry Stimson, Secretary of War Frank Knox and President Roosevelt, who were all impressed with the craft's performance.

A convalescent hospital was established at the camp in 1942, and several thousand WAAC (Women's Army Auxiliary Corps) nurses were trained there before being posted overseas. Antisubmarine reconnaissance missions took off from the two runways known as Otis Field.

In July 1943, a mock German village was built at the camp for soldiers to practice the type of close combat they would encounter once Germany was invaded. The village of "Deutschendorf" consisted of fifteen buildings, including a beer hall, bakery, school and barbershop, where wooden silhouettes of enemy soldiers (many resembling Hitler himself) would pop up from their various hiding places. The following year would see the arrival of actual German soldiers at the POW camp established there. At war's end, thousands of returning GIs were processed and discharged at the camp.

Camp Myles Standish

Thirty-six families were evicted from their homes in order to build this camp on 1,600 acres in the city of Taunton. Construction began in June 1942 and was completed in time for an October opening. The camp could accommodate twenty thousand personnel and was the third largest in the state after Edwards and Devens.

Camp Myles Standish was used as a staging area for troops and equipment from across the country. Soldiers would pass through for just a few days and then board trains for the Boston Port of Embarkation (BPOE) before shipping to overseas posts. The regular arrival and departure by train of troops and equipment made for a busy place, with over one million service members passing through during the war. In March 1944, captured Italian soldiers arrived at the camp as members of Italian Service Units (ISU), a status applied to those soldiers after the surrender of Italy in September 1943.

The hectic activity continued as the war was ending, and thousands of soldiers arrived to be discharged before traveling back to their home states.

Main gate at Camp Myles Standish. *NARA*.

Returning GIs would spend between twenty-four and forty-eight hours at the camp, just enough time to make a phone call, send a telegram, exchange foreign currency or grab a beer. Other facilities at the camp included a library, chapel, movie theater and dry-cleaning station. Returning troopships no longer landed in Boston after the last week of December 1945, and the camp closed as a staging area on New Year's Day 1946.

BOSTON ARMY BASE

Located on fifty-eight acres on the South Boston waterfront, the army base was located in a 1.5-million-square-foot building constructed as the Boston Army Supply Base in 1918. The base employed fifty thousand civilian and military workers during the war. In April 1942, the area was designated as the Boston Port of Embarkation and was a transit hub for millions of tons of military cargo, as well as thousands of servicemen, most arriving from Camp Myles Standish in Taunton before shipping overseas. Ships regularly departed the port bearing food, ammunition and medical supplies. The dry dock was one of the world's longest and was used for repairs.

After the base closed, the City of Boston acquired a large portion of the property and created the Boston Marine Industrial Park, now known as the Raymond L. Flynn Marine Park. Cruise ships frequently docked here at the former Black Falcon Cruise Terminal.

NAVAL AIR STATION SQUANTUM

Prior to World War II, the area in Quincy known as Squantum Point had been an airfield for biplanes and was home first to the Harvard Aeronautical Society, then a destroyer plant operated by Bethlehem Steel in the waning days of World War I. It was a naval reserve air base between the wars and, beginning in 1941, became a fully operational naval air station. The base provided training for both navy and marine pilots, as well as pilots from the British Royal Air Force (RAF). Navy squadrons stationed there regularly flew antisubmarine patrols off Boston Harbor and points north. Joseph Kennedy Jr., son of the former ambassador to Great Britain and brother of John, future thirty-fifth president, received his initial flight training at Squantum in July 1941. Kennedy was killed while flying in a mission over England in August 1944.

SOUTH WEYMOUTH NAVAL AIR STATION

In early 1942, the threat of German U-boat attack in the Atlantic was at its highest. Merchant ships, silhouetted by the lights of coastal cities, were easy targets; in the first three weeks of January, thirty-five Allied merchant ships and one British destroyer were sunk by subs off the New England coast. The previous October, the navy had begun construction of a blimp station in order to monitor and defend the attacks. The South Weymouth Naval Air Station was ready for service the following spring, three months ahead of schedule.

The South Weymouth site joined a station at Lakehurst, New Jersey, as part of the navy's Lighter Than Air (LTA) program of coastal defense. The 1,200-acre site, which included parts of Abington and Rockland, was

Hangar One at South Weymouth Naval Air Station, December 1942. Note the size of the cars parked in front of the row of windows. *NARA.*

K-38 makes an emergency landing at South Weymouth Naval Air Station, 1943. *NARA.*

dedicated on March 1. Opening ceremonies included the arrival of an airship from Lakehurst, crewed by Domenic Fusile of Medford, which hovered over the ceremony before dropping a congratulatory note to the new station commander. The station would be the home of Airship Patrol Squadron Eleven-Z (ZP-11). The squadron consisted of eight ZNP-K ships and two ZZN-G ships. Each K airship was 252 feet long with a 49-foot control cabin and was manned by a crew of ten. Each carried four depth bombs and two machine guns. To accommodate the squadron, two blimp hangars were built; Hangar One housed six blimps and was 956 feet wide and 150 feet tall, covering four acres.

The ability of blimps to fly low for long distances made them extremely useful in protecting convoys of merchant ships. There are no recorded attacks by blimps on U-boats, but their presence certainly frustrated German efforts to sink Allied ships in the Atlantic. Blimp patrols were also used in search-and-rescue efforts of ships that had come under U-boat attack.

In the summer of 1944, a blimp from South Weymouth went down off the coast of Maine, and to this day, the incident is a source of mystery and controversy. The K-14 took off from South Weymouth on Sunday morning, July 2, and headed north on routine patrol. The crew checked in by radio at 9:30 p.m., but after they failed to make contact at their next scheduled time, boats, blimps and planes began their search efforts. The blimp was finally located by a navy patrol boat at about 5:00 a.m. east of Mount Desert Island and south of Bar Harbor. Four survivors were clinging to the wreckage. Among the missing was Andover resident William Hugo. William McDonnell of Braintree and Ensign Ernest Sharp of North Abington both survived. The rescue team picked up the survivors, and the blimp's wreckage was towed first to Bunkers Cove on Little Cranberry Island and then to the coast guard base at Southwest Harbor.

Although the navy investigation determined the cause of the crash to be pilot error, some believe the blimp was shot down by German U-*233*, which was reportedly in the area at the time and was sunk just a few days later off the coast of Nova Scotia. Witnesses to the salvage operation later described watching the blimp being spread out, revealing multiple bullet holes.

CLOSE CALL FOR THE *LARK*

The presence of blimp patrols did not discourage all U-boat activity; in 1944, a local fishing crew had a narrow escape off the coast of Nova Scotia. The trawler *Lark* left Boston on June 5, its twenty-six-man crew captained by thirty-year-old James Abbott of Dorchester. In the early morning hours of the thirteenth, the trawler was fifty miles off McNutt Island when Abbott saw a ship about three hundred feet away. Thinking it was a Canadian patrol boat, he went below deck, leaving crew member John Aspell at the wheel. Moments later, a frantic Aspell was shouting to his captain that the ship they had seen was a submarine, and to punctuate his announcement, a shell from the sub came flying across the ship's bow. After firing a barrage of machine gun fire through the fishing boat's rigging, the U-boat disappeared. At this point, the crew, with the exception of Abbott, seventy-four-year-old ship's cook Daniel Maloney and Rex, the ship's dog, abandoned ship and boarded five dories.

For the next fifteen minutes, the sub attacked the *Lark* with both shells and machine gun fire. Abbott took cover behind the remaining dories, lying flat on the deck, at times praying aloud while the submarine circled the besieged *Lark*. One shell ripped through the pilothouse close to where Abbott had been standing just moments before. When the shelling finally stopped and the submarine disappeared, Abbott found Maloney in the forecastle dressed in his best outfit with a survival package of bread, molasses and water, ready to abandon ship.

The crew in the dories then rowed back to the boat, not before their own close encounter with the sub. The U-boat was so close to one dory that it bumped into and broke the oar being held by crew member Herman

Left: Damage to the pilothouse of the *Lark* from a German shell. *NARA*.

Opposite: *Lark* crew member Howard Bichard holds the oar that came in contact with the U-*107* as it submerged. *NARA*.

Bichard. Miraculously, none of the crew was hurt, and the *Lark* was still seaworthy. Mechanic Bill McKenzie of Saugus made repairs, and they set off for home with their haul of 105,000 pounds of cod, hake and pollock intact, both pumps working to keep the water out. They arrived in Boston two days later and, after telling their story at a press conference, were hailed as heroes. Inspection of the damage revealed over five hundred bullet holes in the ship's sails. This was the second U-boat encounter for crew member James Doucette of Lynn. In 1918, Doucette had been aboard the schooner *A. Platt Andrew* when it was attacked and sunk by a German submarine, forcing the crew to row forty-five miles in dories to Nova Scotia. It was later revealed that the attack on the *Lark* came from U-*107* under the command of Captain Volker Simmermacher. U-*107* was sunk by a British air patrol off the coast of France in August with a loss of all hands.

BOSTON HARBOR DEFENSES

During the war, there were close to twenty military installations on the harbor islands and in coastal towns from Scituate on the South Shore to Nahant on the North Shore. These defenses included antisubmarine and antitorpedo nets, army mines, navy sonar–type detectors and an antisub magnetic loop on the harbor seabed. Coastal beaches and shores were covered with barbed wire and patrolled by coast guard sentries and trained dogs. Gun batteries were placed strategically on harbor island locations, and surface vessels routinely patrolled the area.

In June 1942, the operator of the minefield at Fort Warren noticed unusual activity in the southern channel of Boston Harbor. Soon, the harbor defense system was on full alert, and a search was made for any vessels in the harbor, but none was found. Later inspection revealed one of the mines bearing propeller marks. It wasn't until years after the war that the full explanation for the incident would come to light.

The release of declassified German documents in the 1950s confirmed that in June 1942, the submarine U-*87* laid six magnetic mines in the shipping lanes of Boston Harbor. U-*87* then went on to sink three freighters before being sunk off the coast of Cape Cod in 1943. Despite the army dimout order extending three miles from the coast and encompassing a twelve-mile radius of Boston City Hall, the U-boat captain noted in his log that Boston was "hardly darkened." In April 1960, an officer from the naval reserve discovered the existence of the mines and expressed concern that they could be a danger to small boats and scuba divers in the harbor. A search by two naval minesweepers found two rusting baby carriages but no mines.

Boston Navy Yard

The United States government now calls on the historic Boston Navy Yard to do its part again by building the warships that will protect America and our free way of life. The Navy Yard is pledged to build these war vessels faster and better than ever before so that victory may be won as soon as possible.
—from "Working Together in the Boston Navy Yard" employee handbook, 1942

The Boston Navy Yard (also known as the Charlestown Shipyard and Boston Naval Shipyard) was the oldest military site in the state, established in 1800 at the confluence of the Mystic and Charles Rivers in Boston's inner harbor. It had been repairing, refitting and building ships for American sailors from the War of 1812 through World War I. The frigate USS *Constitution*, whose construction predates the founding of the shipyard, has been docked there since 1897. ("Old Ironsides" was named the symbolic flagship of the U.S.

Left: Boston Navy Yard employee handbook, 1943. *Author's collection.*

Right: A page from the navy yard employee handbook describing the dress code for women. *Author's collection.*

fleet during the Second World War. Shortly after the attack on Pearl Harbor, it was proposed that the iconic ship be moved to a safer location, but that idea was eventually abandoned.)

Destroyer production began at the navy yard in 1932. In September 1940, when fifty World War I–era destroyers were transferred to the Royal Navy under Roosevelt's plan to swap ships for land leases from Great Britain, the navy yard workers took on the job of updating and refurbishing the first group of these ships. Shortly after Pearl Harbor, the yard began building the new destroyer escort class of destroyers. These ships were designed to escort convoys of merchant ships across the Atlantic. They were smaller than conventional destroyers, faster, less expensive to build and required a smaller crew. Also constructed at the yard were two types of landing craft, the Landing Craft, Mechanized (LCM) and Landing Ship, Tank (LST).

Over the course of the war, the yard employed some fifty thousand workers, 15 to 20 percent of them women performing jobs that had traditionally been done by men, such as welding and pipe fitting. From 1941 to 1945, over six thousand vessels were launched from the navy yard. At the height of their productivity, workers had reduced the construction time of a destroyer from one year to just three months. While the navy yard was the workplace of thousands of local workers, it was also a naval base housing hundreds of navy officers, sailors and marines. The navy yard closed in 1975 after almost 175 years of operation.

FORE RIVER SHIPYARD

The shipyard had been located at Quincy Point since 1901, producing a number of navy ships over the years. From 1913 to 1963, it was owned and operated by Bethlehem Steel. Ninety-two ships were built there during World War II, including battleships, destroyers, destroyer escorts, cruisers and carriers. During that period, over thirty-two thousand workers were employed, two thousand of them women.

The USS *Massachusetts* was built at the shipyard; construction started in 1939, and the battleship was launched on September 23, 1941. After undergoing sea trials off the coast of Maine, "Big Mamie" was ready for service and took part in the invasion of French North Africa in November 1942. The USS *Lexington* is another significant ship built there. The 820-foot carrier was laid down in July 1941 and launched in September 1942. The *Lexington* saw extensive action in the Pacific.

"KILROY WAS HERE"

"Kilroy was here" began as a military phenomenon, a piece of graffiti soldiers and sailors would leave to mark their presence and add a bit of humor to the grim circumstances of battle. The phrase, often accompanied by a cartoon drawing of a bald, long-nosed character peering over a wall, began appearing in mid-war in a variety of places in the European theater. The graffiti was found on bridges, tanks, bombs, the walls of bombed-out homes and every available surface a GI could imagine. The phrase quickly became popular on the homefront, where it was found in animated cartoons, doodled on the covers of student notebooks and in musical form on at least two jazz recordings. It was even the subject of a 1947 movie starring Jackie Cooper and Jackie Coogan. When the National World War II Memorial in Washington, D.C., was dedicated in 2004, the phrase was etched into the stone pillars in two hidden places.

Historians have conjectured that the graffiti was an American version of an earlier character named Smoe or Chad, drawn by British servicemen, but at war's end, dozens of returning servicemen claimed to be the real Kilroy, with several of those claimants living right here in Massachusetts.

The first candidate was Sergeant Francis Kilroy of Everett. According to a *Globe* article from November 1945, Kilroy was stationed at the army airfield in Boca Raton, Florida, when a bout of flu sent him to the infirmary for a time. To cheer up the ailing sergeant, his friend Jimmy Maloney wrote, "Kilroy will be here next week" on a bulletin board. A month later, the recovered sergeant shipped out to Italy, where he was greeted by the now familiar phrase written in hundreds of places, the work of his friend Maloney and countless imitators.

The Everett sergeant enjoyed a brief period of local fame, but the rest of the nation, unaware of his claim, remained obsessed with finding the truth behind the Kilroy phenomenon. Newspapers in dozens of states published letters from citizens claiming to know the identity of the real Kilroy. The American Transit Association and the Boston Elevated Railway Company attempted to settle the issue once and for all in December 1946 when it ran a contest offering the prize of a twenty-ton 1910 model streetcar to the writer of the most convincing essay proving their true Kilroy identity.

Kilroy was found just about everywhere during the war, including on this promotional button for war bonds. *Author's collection.*

The winner of the contest was James J. Kilroy, a forty-four-year-old father of nine from Halifax. Kilroy claimed that when he started working at the Fore River Shipyard two days before the attack on Pearl Harbor, he would write the phrase on ship parts in his capacity as an inspector. He also wrote it on the bulkheads of the ships *Lexington*, *Baltimore* and *Massachusetts*, which were built at the shipyard. The Kilroy family took delivery of their prize just before Christmas 1946. The trolley car was attached to their home and used for sleeping quarters for six of the nine Kilroy children.

Kilroy Square in Quincy Center, 2023. *Photo by author.*

The results of the essay contest made national headlines, and over time, James Kilroy's story has been accepted by many as the definitive explanation of the phrase. The city of Quincy has no doubt who the authentic Kilroy was. In 2021, a new retail center named Kilroy Square opened in the downtown area. The true spirit of Kilroy, however, was captured in this editorial from the November 25, 1946 edition of the Stockton (CA) *Evening and Sunday Record*: "[Kilroy's] identity really is of little consequence. People all over the world know who the real Kilroy was. He was personified in the American fighting man whose valor and industry defied the dictators who believed Kilroy couldn't get 'here' and if he did, he couldn't stay."

HINGHAM

The seaside town of Hingham was a remarkably busy place during the war years, with thousands of civilians and military personnel engaged in a variety of activities. The town's coastal location and proximity to facilities in nearby Quincy and South Weymouth made it an essential site in the war effort. The Hingham Naval Ammunition Depot was established in 1903 and was in full operation beginning in 1941. Later that year, two additional facilities were built nearby: the Hingham Naval Ammunition Depot Annex and the Bethlehem Steel Shipyard. The annex began operations in October 1941 and was used to store and safeguard ammunition farther inland. Approximately one thousand acres along the Weymouth Back River were taken and 240 families were evicted before construction began. The system of concrete bunkers was located two miles from the older depot and connected by a railroad spur. The ammunition depot was closed in 1961 and remained U.S. Army property until it was turned over to the Town of Hingham in 1972.

Hingham Shipyard

Bethlehem Steel, which operated the Quincy Shipyard at Fore River, also operated a shipyard at nearby Hingham at the mouth of the Weymouth Back River, where as many as twenty-three thousand workers built destroyer escorts. Ground was broken for the 129-acre facility in February 1942; the first keel was laid in June, and the first launch took place in September. Speed was the hallmark of this operation; sixteen keels were laid in one day in 1942. In its three years of operation, the shipyard produced over 200 destroyers and landing craft. The 227th and last ship to be built there was the USS *Frankovich*, commissioned on September 7, 1945.

After the war, part of the shipyard was used as a naval warehouse, and sales of surplus equipment were routinely held. In 1963, entrepreneur Jerry Ellis opened a retail store in one of the many buildings on the property, selling surplus and insurance lots as he had been doing for years. Ellis named his business after the original shipyard number designation still affixed to the side of the warehouse, and thus the Building #19 store was born. The Building #19 franchise eventually included ten stores and was a Massachusetts institution until its closure in 2013.

Harbor Defenses of New Bedford

A system of coastal defenses, including guns, submarine nets, minefields, fire control towers and other deterrents, was established at various locations on the southeastern shore of Massachusetts. The main purpose of these defenses was to protect the Cape Cod Canal. Fort Rodman, located on Clark's Point in New Bedford, was a nineteenth-century stone fort that became the primary installation in the coastal defense of the Buzzard's Bay waterways. Beginning before the war, gun batteries were installed, and soldiers mobilized at many strategic locations on the coast and on nearby islands. Some of these sites included Cuttyhunk, Naushon and Nashawena Islands, Butler's Point in Marion, Gooseberry Neck in Westport, Mishaum Point in Dartmouth and Sagamore Hill Military Reservation, situated at the northern end of the canal. The remains of World War II–era construction can still be found at many of these sites.

WATERTOWN ARSENAL

When war broke out in 1941, the Watertown Arsenal had been developing, building and testing weapons for 125 years. The war years saw a great expansion in both the size of the physical plant as well as the workforce; by the end of 1942, the facility covered one hundred acres and employed over ten thousand people. Among the weapons crafted there were antiaircraft guns, shell casings, gun carriages and railway guns. A great milestone was reached in February 1944, when the arsenal produced its 100,000[th] gun. The event was part of a live NBC radio broadcast. In late 1944, the arsenal experienced a serious manpower shortage. The facility needed another eight hundred workers to work on the production of 240-millimeter shell casings. The need was so great that a direct plea was made by soldiers who had recently fought in Europe. Five veterans arrived at the plant and described the difficulty in fighting the Germans when shells had to be rationed. Despite the manpower shortage, the arsenal was regularly awarded the coveted Army-Navy E Award for productivity. The facility closed in 1968 and today is the site of a retail, residential and business community.

SPRINGFIELD ARMORY

An arsenal was established at Springfield in 1777 during the American Revolution, and production of weapons began here in 1795. The armory would manufacture and supply weapons to U.S. armed forces for the next 174 years. From 1936 to 1945, over 3.5 million M-1 rifles were manufactured in Springfield. The rifle was standard issue for every branch of the service and was called "the greatest battle implement ever devised" by General George S. Patton. At its peak in 1945, the workforce numbered over thirteen thousand, many of whom were women ordnance workers.

WESTOVER AIR BASE

In December 1939, it was announced that an army air base would be built on over four thousand acres in Chicopee. The base was named after Major General Oscar Westover, who had been killed in a crash in California the previous year. Construction started in February 1940 on the former tobacco farm. Events in Europe in the spring speeded up the project, and by July, the first battalion had arrived. It was the largest military air facility in the region, serving as an embarkation/debarkation point, a bomber training base and a base for antisubmarine air patrols.

CAMP FRAMINGHAM

The one-hundred-acre site off Concord Street had been known as the Musterfield since the state established a camp there in 1872 for the Massachusetts Volunteer Militia (today's National Guard). The site was a staging area for United States forces in the Spanish-American War, the 1916 Mexican War and World War I. In May 1942, troops from the army's 131st Combat Engineering Battalion arrived to prepare the site for their stay as part of the coastal defense system. New buildings were designed to look like those of a typical New England village in order to fool enemy bombers. The barracks resembled Colonial homes, the headquarters looked like a school and the auditorium appeared as a church. In September 1943, the battalion shipped out to the Pacific, where the men served in Guam and the Philippines.

CUSHING GENERAL HOSPITAL

Cushing General Hospital was built on 110 acres in the southwest section of Framingham near Farm Pond and close to the railroad line. Construction began in April 1943, and the facility was dedicated on January 24, 1944. It was named for Dr. Harvey Cushing, a brilliant neurosurgeon who taught at Harvard Medical School and had served as a colonel in France during the First World War.

The compound contained ninety-five semipermanent buildings, including medical facilities, patient housing, administration headquarters, barracks for staff, warehouses, recreation halls and a chapel. Hospital trains arrived from Boston on a regular basis. Originally built to service 1,750 patients, the hospital grew in both size and population as the war escalated and at its peak housed some 3,000 war wounded. Approximately 1,000 military personnel and several hundred civilians as well as countless local volunteers worked at Cushing. After the war, the facility operated as a veterans' hospital and then an elder care facility before closing for good in 1991.

MAYNARD AMMUNITION DEPOT

The towns of Hudson, Maynard, Stow and Sudbury are about twenty-four miles from the coast, a safe enough distance for an ammunition storage facility. In March 1942, the army informed families living in those towns that their farms and homes would be confiscated and the land, covering over four square miles, would be transformed into a network of railroad lines connecting fifty-five concrete bunkers built into the sides of man-made earthen hills. Approximately 139 families, mostly farmers of Finnish descent, were displaced. The *Globe* reported that the general feeling of those displaced was that of acceptance and willingness to help the government in the war effort. In October 2005, the site was dedicated as the Assabet River National Wildlife Refuge.

Cushing General Hospital in Framingham, March 1944. *NARA.*

One of more than fifty concrete ammunition bunkers at the Maynard Ammunition Depot. *NARA.*

POW CAMPS

American success on the battlefield created a need for the internment of captured prisoners. Japanese prisoners were sent to camps on the West Coast, while Italian and German POWs were mostly housed in camps on the East Coast.

POWS were held at Fort Devens, Camp Edwards and Camp Myles Standish and in Boston at Camp McKay and Fort Andrews. Beginning in 1943, both German and Italian prisoners of war were held at Fort Devens. Five thousand POWs were brought there, making it New England's largest POW camp. The prisoners were treated fairly and in accordance with Geneva Convention guidelines, publishing their own newspaper, attending college classes and even working at farms and apple orchards in Middlesex and Worcester Counties. German prisoners from Rommel's Afrika Korps arrived at Camp Edwards in June 1944. Under careful supervision and close watch, they were hired out to assist with both the cranberry and strawberry harvest. In September 1944, an unnamed hurricane swept through the East, leaving thousands of downed trees, which the POWs helped save as board timber.

Camp McKay, Boston. *NARA*.

Italian Service Units working at the Boston Port of Embarkation. *NARA.*

Camp Myles Standish housed as many as two thousand prisoners, mostly Italians. A grotto honoring the Virgin Mary built by Italian POWs still stands in the industrial park that was developed on the old campground. Italian prisoners gained a special status after Italy surrendered in September 1943. They were now classified as "co-belligerents," and although not technically free, they were permitted many more liberties than their German counterparts, such as the freedom to attend church and social events. Many from Camp McKay worked at the Boston Port of Embarkation, loading supplies onto Liberty ships bound for Europe.

ESCAPES

Escapes were common, but prisoners in POW outfits with limited English had few options, and most were recaptured within days or even hours of their escape.

In May 1944, two German soldiers who had escaped from Fort Devens were quickly captured in the town of Harvard. As a posse of some 250 armed police and volunteers combed the farms and swamps four miles from the camp, fifty-five-year-old Mrs. Jessie Davenport heard voices speaking in a foreign language outside her kitchen window. After hearing a loud sneeze, she decided to call the police.

Twenty-three-year-old Heinz Jacob managed to escape three times in one year. In April 1944, he walked from a work detail at Fort Devens, hitchhiked to Boston and found time to romance a young Back Bay woman who eventually turned him in. He escaped from Devens again in November and spent several days in New York before being captured. His third escape came in September 1945, when he left a work detail at a camp in Spencer Lake, Maine, and was apprehended near the Canadian border a few days later.

Such stories were commonplace in the towns surrounding the camps, but one escape saga stands out for its daring and its longevity. Fritz Kamerdiner escaped from Devens on December 23, 1944, and was not recaptured until July 1946 in Nantucket. He had spent time in New York working as a carpenter and passing himself off as Swiss-French. It is believed he had made the acquaintance of a woman who was suspected of fraternizing with him while she was a civilian worker at Devens. After the German surrender, many POWs attempted escape to avoid being returned to their home countries.

A CAPTAIN IS CAPTURED

Friedrich Steinhoff was a German U-boat captain who was captured after he surrendered his boat, the U-873, about five hundred miles off Newfoundland just one week after the German surrender. Steinhoff, his crew and his submarine were taken to the naval base at Portsmouth, New Hampshire, on May 13, 1945, where the fifty-four officers and crew members were processed. They were then driven on buses to Boston and briefly held at the Hotel Buckminster in Kenmore Square. A crowd of several hundred gathered and shouted, "Kill them" and "Shoot them" as they exited the buses and marched under marine guard into the hotel. From the hotel, the captured Germans were transported a mile or so to the Charles Street Jail and mixed in with the general population. Not surprisingly, the other prisoners tormented them. At some point, Steinhoff was able to break his sunglasses and use the sharpened lens to slice his wrists. He died at Mass General Hospital and is buried at the Fort Devens cemetery along with twenty Italian prisoners.

Captain Friedrich Steinhoff and the crew of the captured U-873 in Portsmouth, New Hampshire, May 1945. Captain Steinhoff is seen wearing a white cap with his hands folded behind his back. *NARA*.

Hotel Buckminster, Kenmore Square, Boston. *Author's collection*.

Chapter 5

CELEBRATION/CONCLUSION

By the late summer of 1943, military leaders were assuring citizens that the war was in its final phase and that complete and final victory for Allied forces was only a matter of time. Recent victories on every front prompted General George C. Marshall to declare that upcoming offenses would eventually lead to the absolute defeat of the Axis. The successful invasion of Sicily in July resulted in the arrest of Mussolini and the retreat of thousands of German soldiers from Italy. The plane-spotting program had ended, and dimout regulations were easing. It was during this time that British prime minister Winston Churchill made a secret visit to Cambridge.

Churchill, who had been staying at the White House for talks with FDR, arrived in Boston under heavy security and secrecy on September 6, before proceeding to Harvard University in Cambridge, where he was to receive an honorary doctor of laws degree. The president and fellows of the college had voted the previous May to confer the degree on the prime minister, allowing him to accept the honor at his convenience, rather than at the traditional spring commencement.

The day before the visit, news outlets, including the Boston papers, announced that Churchill would be giving a speech in an unnamed American city to be broadcast over live radio, but it was expected to be "of no political significance." Churchill; his wife, Winnie; and their daughter Mary arrived at Sanders Theater on the Harvard campus for the event described simply as "An Academic Meeting." Faculty and dignitaries in attendance for the occasion were surprised and delighted when they discovered the identity of the guest of honor.

British prime minister Winston Churchill addresses the crowd at Harvard University while Governor Leverett Saltonstall looks on. *Courtesy of the Boston Public Library, Leslie Jones Collection.*

After receiving his LLD degree from Harvard president James Conant, Churchill addressed the audience of 1,300, acknowledging the progress of the war and the tasks yet to be accomplished. His talk focused on American-British cooperation and partnership and the need for a transition to "Basic English" to facilitate ease of communication between nations.

At the conclusion of his speech, the British leader made his way to the steps of Memorial Church, where some seven thousand sailors and soldiers studying at Harvard had gathered in formation in the yard. The military students studying at the college had been informed of the visit beforehand and sworn to secrecy. Churchill addressed the servicemen briefly, banging his cane on the ground for emphasis and giving his famous "V for Victory" salute. He then returned to Washington to continue his talks with Roosevelt, leaving behind lasting memories and more. It was reported that the cigar stubs left by the chain-smoking prime minister were scooped up out of the ashtrays in President Conant's house as souvenirs by members of the housekeeping staff.

Italy Surrenders

While the prime minister was addressing the crowd at Sanders Theater, he was sitting on some very big news. Just three days prior, on September 3, Italy had surrendered. The public would have to wait until September 8 for the official announcement.

In Boston, Cambridge and other cities, the surrender was announced over speakers tied into the air raid warning system. The Boston police safety car drove through the streets of the city with an officer repeating over the loudspeakers, "Italy has surrendered!" Fire bells and church bells rang across the state, and joyful residents spontaneously celebrated in the streets. Boston's acting mayor, Thomas Hannon Jr., declared a Day of Jubilation in the city. Italian Americans were especially jubilant, having endured the effects of the alien enemy laws and the suspicions of their neighbors. The announcement came on the same day as the Third War Bond Drive began, and a Filene's ad in the *Globe* encouraged readers to "Buy an extra bond tonight and make Hitler and Hirohito go the way of Italy." The sunset that evening was particularly impressive, with a combination of light rain and scattered clouds reflecting sunlight, causing a vivid display of color that some believed was Mother Nature's way of celebrating the good news. Seymour Getter of Boston summarized the news with a baseball analogy: "This is the lucky seventh, but we've got two more innings to go."

V-E DAY

Italy's surrender was a turning point in the war, but fighting would continue for another year and a half before the Germans surrendered. After German officials signed surrender documents on May 7 and 8, President Truman in a radio address declared May 9 Victory-Europe (V-E) Day. With the war in the Pacific still raging, celebrations across the state were tempered. In the North End's Little Italy, Italian Americans spread the word from balcony to balcony before weeping and dancing in the streets and cafés to toast the victory. In Watertown, the news prompted the sounding of the air raid siren, causing residents to believe it was an actual alarm and snarling traffic in the city for fifteen minutes.

For German POWs at Fort Devens, it was just another workday. Later that week, camp commander Colonel Harold Storke released a written statement from the prisoners that said in part they were looking forward to "a better Germany in a peaceful world" and they welcomed "the end of the National Socialist regime which brought death, want, and tyranny to the German people and to the world."

PATTON'S HOMECOMING

One month after V-E Day, Massachusetts residents got the opportunity to celebrate and release the tensions and anxiety of the past four years when they welcomed home the state's most famous and decorated hero, General George S. Patton. A Californian by birth, Patton had made his home in Massachusetts after marrying the socialite Beatrice Ayer in 1910. Beatrice was the daughter of textile magnate Frederick Ayer, president of the Lawrence-based American Woolen Mills. In 1928, the Pattons moved into an eighteenth-century farmhouse called Green Meadows in Hamilton and spent their summers there when General Patton was not performing military duties in various parts of the world.

Patton had successfully led armored American forces first in North Africa and Sicily and then in Germany during the Battle of the Bulge. He was known for his no-nonsense leadership style and gruff demeanor. The reception for the general was decidedly festive. Patton landed at the airfield in Bedford on June 8 after flying from Paris via Nova Scotia. His motorcade then traveled to Boston, with an estimated one million people lining the streets along the twenty-five-mile route, hoping to get a glimpse of their hero. The general waved to enthusiastic supporters from an open-air car loaned by the Revere Fire Department and driven by Fire Lieutenant Albert Colella.

In Lexington, a colonial town crier announced the general's arrival as he passed the historic town green. In Harvard Square, the motorcade passed under raised fire ladders and moved past hundreds of enthusiastic spectators before ending its journey at the Hatch Shell on the Esplanade, where a crowd of twenty thousand had gathered to hear Patton speak. Included in the crowd were Mayor Kerrigan and Governor Tobin, as well as over three hundred wounded veterans from Cushing Hospital. (In 1953, a statue of Patton was erected at the Hatch Shell to commemorate his appearance.)

Later that night, Patton was honored at a dinner at the Copley Plaza, where he entered the ballroom to the strains of a musical salute to the armed forces written by his wife. While addressing the crowd of dignitaries, "Old Blood and Guts" broke down as he described the courage and determination of the soldiers who had served under him.

General George S. Patton is greeted in Hamilton. *Courtesy of the Boston Public Library, Leslie Jones Collection.*

The next day, the general flew to his hometown of Los Angeles for an even bigger reception. He returned a few weeks later to Hamilton, where the crowd was much smaller and the celebration more subdued. Patton returned to Europe in July to serve in the Occupation Forces. On December 9, the general's limousine collided with an army truck, causing him to strike his head on the partition that separated the driver and passenger compartments. Although it was a low-speed impact, Patton suffered a spinal cord injury that left him paralyzed from the neck down. He died twelve days later on December 21 from a blood clot and was buried with fallen soldiers of his Third Army under a simple white cross in the American Military Cemetery in Hamm, Luxembourg. He was sixty.

V-J Day

At 7:00 p.m. on Tuesday, August 14, President Truman announced the Japanese surrender. As word spread and it became clear that the news was not just another rumor, the city of Boston erupted into a "joyous madhouse" that made the celebration in 1918 look like "a flea circus," according to the *Globe*. Impromptu parades sprang up in every town, with children blowing noisemakers and banging pots and pans or anything they could find to join in the celebrations. By 10:30 that night, an estimated 750,000 people had filled the streets of downtown Boston. Auto horns blared and church bells rang, and a controlled pandemonium took over the city. The following day was declared a holiday, and the celebration continued in Boston and across the state. Kegs of beer flowed freely in the streets. Servicemen, their lips and cheeks covered with lipstick marks, were especially enthusiastic, frolicking on the Common and tossing unsuspecting female revelers into the frog pond. One drunken sailor climbed out of a fifth-floor window of the Hotel Touraine and danced on the ledge until a level-headed companion pulled him back in. Accidents were inevitable with such large crowds carousing with abandon in the streets; over 150 people were admitted to city hospitals with injuries ranging from cuts and scratches to bones fractured by collisions with autos. Many people chose to celebrate in a more contemplative way by gathering in churches to pray.

Similar celebrations took place in cities and towns across the state. In Greenfield, residents held hands and danced in the street by the light of flares and the sound of exploding firecrackers. Decorated automobiles paraded down the streets of Fitchburg with joyful occupants hanging out windows, sitting on hoods and balancing on bumpers and running boards. By day's end, city streets across the state were littered with confetti, streamers and other remnants of the night's festivities.

Governor Maurice Tobin spoke in the State House's Hall of Flags praising the more than 500,000 Massachusetts men and women who served, over 10,000 of whom gave the final sacrifice:

> *The epic of valor thus written by the men of Massachusetts—and the men of every other state in the union—is an epic to be treasured by us and by a grateful mankind throughout all future generations. And let us never forget that the most memorable pages of that story were written in the blood of upstanding lads who left their beloved homes never to return again—heroes who gave to the last full measure of devotion that peace and freedom might be guaranteed to men of goodwill, not only in America but the world over.*

LITTLE MISTER VICTORY

Amid the chaotic celebrations, sixteen-year-old Charlie Sparato left his home in East Boston and arrived at the Common to begin his afternoon shift selling newspapers by the entrance to the subway. Shortly after arriving, Sparato was approached by a well-dressed young woman of about twenty-five, carrying an infant no more than a few weeks old. The woman asked Charlie if he would hold the child for just a few minutes while she made a phone call. She handed him two one-dollar bills and disappeared into the crowd.

Thirty minutes went by, and the woman had not returned. Anxious to get to his post and begin his shift, Charlie enlisted the aid of three young women from Dorchester who took the baby boy and waited for the woman's return. When it became evident that she was not coming back, the girls found Charlie and walked to the Joy Street police station, where they told their story to officers on duty. The search was on for the mysterious young woman who handed over an infant during the biggest celebration Boston had ever seen.

While police investigated the few clues they had, the baby was brought to Boston City Hospital for an examination. The dark-haired, blue-eyed, eight-pound baby boy was found to be approximately five weeks old and in good health. He was well dressed in a white dress and pink booties. Nurses at the hospital gave the baby several nicknames, including "Douglas" after General MacArthur and "Little Mister Victory." Police made impressions of his footprints to take to area hospitals in an attempt to find a match. Newspapers across the country carried the story over the next few weeks, revealing new clues as they were uncovered, such as the initials "T.M.K" embroidered on the shirt the baby was wearing. Tips came in leading authorities from the Back Bay to Long Island, to Portland, Maine, but they all proved to be dead ends. After a few weeks, the story faded from headlines, and the fate of "Little Mister Victory" became lost to time.

In 2005, on the sixtieth anniversary of V-J Day, an article in the *Globe* retold the story of Little Mister Victory and contemplated his whereabouts at age sixty. The article prompted a letter to the paper from Charlie Sparato himself, now seventy-six years old and living in California. Charlie's letter corrected some details from the original 1945 story and closed with the plea, "I would like to meet Mr. Victory if that's possible. Mr. Victory, where are you?" Those familiar with the story have asked the same question for years and are hopeful that the mystery will one day be solved.

Return to Normalcy

On August 25, all rationing, except for sugar, was suspended. That same week, the DuPont Lucite plant in Leominster closed, leaving 325 employees out of work. In the weeks that followed, some 200,000 munitions workers in New England would lose their jobs as the nation shifted to a peacetime economy. Soldiers and sailors came home by the thousands, many accompanied by war brides from England, Australia and several other countries.

As service members began returning home, a serious situation arose concerning the thousands of war souvenirs stuffed into duffel bags and foot lockers that made their way into homes across the state. Along with banners, flags, photos, ticket stubs, swords and pistols were potentially deadly projectiles. (A Trophy Retention Certificate issued to my father in October 1945 lists a hand grenade and a .50-millimeter mortar shell; I never saw the hand grenade, and the shell was kept in an old Candy Cupboard chocolate box in the bottom drawer of his dresser.) In September, less than a month after V-E Day, the First Naval District along with state and local police launched a statewide campaign to warn of the dangers of live ammunition and explosives to veterans and their families. Returning GI

George Pappageorge lost a thumb and two fingers when a shell detonator he had taken home exploded. A twenty-one-year-old New Bedford man accidentally shot and killed his friend while showing him a .32-caliber souvenir German revolver. In Somerville, a group of boys shot off a stolen phosphorus parachute flare in a neighborhood where it landed on a rooftop, starting a fire that severely damaged the house. The Massachusetts War Trophy Safety Committee warned veterans in 1948 that war souvenirs could kill upward of ten thousand people if not secured safely in the home. Veterans were encouraged to bring their trophies to local police or fire stations to have them "delivened." Many towns had their own committees set up, such as the Norwood War Safeties Committee, which continued to inspect souvenirs for several years after the war's end.

Ted Williams returned to the Red Sox for the 1946 season and led his team to the American League pennant, leading the league in batting and home runs and winning his first MVP award. In the World Series, the Sox lost to the St. Louis Cardinals in seven games and would not make it back to the series for another twenty-one years. In 1950, Williams would once again leave the Red Sox for war, this time serving as a fighter pilot in Korea, where he downed seven enemy airplanes and was awarded the Distinguished Flying Cross.

Over the next few years, the Commonwealth's cities and towns began to honor their war dead. Memorials were erected on town commons, and names were inscribed on walls of honor in city halls. Highways, bridges, tunnels and squares were named for the fallen and remain today to remind us of their sacrifice.

CONCLUSION

The final toll of the war left over 300,000 Americans dead on six continents. It wasn't until October 19, 1947, that the first war dead arrived back in the States. Memorial services to honor the state's fallen were held on Boston Common on October 20; 91 Massachusetts service members were among the first to be repatriated, and over the next few years, from Milton to North Adams, the remains of thousands of Massachusetts natives were returned to their families.

In February 1948, in Dedham, the military funeral of PFC Anthony Palermo, killed at Normandy, held the same pomp and ceremony usually reserved for fallen generals and government leaders. Palermo's casket was placed on the same caisson that had carried the body of President Franklin Roosevelt three years earlier. Drawn by four white horses, the caisson processed solemnly through town, from the funeral home, past Palermo's childhood home to St. Mary's Church, accompanied by an honor guard of VFW and American Legion officers, commanders and chaplains. At the graveside, a volley of rifles was followed by the playing of "Taps." Similar ceremonies took place in Springfield as family members gathered at the train station to receive their loved ones, often accompanied by an honor guard from local veterans' groups and Legion members. These scenes mirrored those earlier scenes of draftees marching to train stations after their induction ceremonies.

There were no parades to honor the citizen army that fought on the homefront, no uniforms to take off and hang in closets, no medal ceremonies for enduring food shortages, travel restrictions and a host of other disruptions to daily life. As families welcomed back familiar routines and familiar faces, there was a great feeling of relief, coupled with the overwhelming sense of loss for those who did not come back. What was well understood and celebrated by all was that a great victory had been achieved, and that victory was won through the combined efforts of every citizen in the Commonwealth.

One Family's Story

Raymond Hickey was born in Framingham on February 28, 1922, to John, a patrolman on the Framingham police force, and Mary McLellan Hickey, a housewife. Older brother John was born in 1920. When Raymond was about three years old, his parents moved a few blocks north from Clark Street to Arthur Street, into an eight-year-old house in the style of a New England four-square. The house on Arthur Street had a good-sized living room with French doors and large windows that allowed lots of light into the home. Upstairs were three bedrooms; as the younger brother, Raymond may have gotten the small bedroom in the southeast corner of the house, facing the backyard and the garage, or he may have bunked with big brother John in the larger bedroom across the hall. The master bedroom was at the top of the stairs facing the street. The backyard was long and flat, a good size for two boys to run and play games in. The neighborhood was a working-class one, with many of the residents employed by the Dennison

Manufacturing Company just a few blocks away. There were a few other children in the neighborhood for the Hickey boys to play with, including Ray's next-door neighbor and classmate Walter O'Donnell.

Ray left high school after three years and was working in a metal shop in town in December 1941. He and his classmate Walter were at the movies when they learned of the attack on Pearl Harbor. In November 1942, Ray enlisted in the U.S. Army Air Corps in Boston and was sent to Scott Field in Illinois to train as a radio operator. After more training in Texas, Arizona, New Mexico and Nebraska, Technical Sergeant Hickey shipped out in December 1943 to an air base in England. There he was assigned as a radioman to a ten-member crew in the 702nd Bomber Squadron, 445th Bomber Group.

On April 12, 1944, the Hickeys received a letter from Raymond describing his nine recent bombing missions over England. Just a few weeks later, a telegram was delivered to the home on Arthur Street: "The Secretary of War desires me to express his deep regret that your son Tech Sergeant Raymond J. Hickey has been reported missing in action since April 13 over Germany. If further details or other information are received, you will be promptly notified." The telegram was signed by Brigadier General Robert Dunlop.

The Hickeys would later learn that their son and his crew took off from Station 124 in England on a bombing mission over Oberpfaffenhofen, Germany. Over their target, they were hit by ground antiaircraft fire and crashed. Raymond's status was updated from Missing in Action to Killed in Action when his body was recovered in Germany. In 1949, Raymond's remains were returned to his family, and he was buried with full military honors in St. Stephen's Cemetery in Framingham. He was posthumously awarded the Purple Heart.

In 1973, Mr. and Mrs. Hickey sold the house on Arthur Street to their surviving son, John, for one dollar. John lived there for the next thirty years and passed away in 2003. In 2004, the house was updated with many modern conveniences while still retaining many of its original features. After being in the Hickey family for almost seventy-five years, it was sold to a new family. Eight years and three more owners later, it was put up for sale once again and purchased in December 2012 by this author. The Hickeys left very few reminders of their longtime residence here: small bits of unburned coal buried in the backyard, a brittle and yellowed permit for a propane stove dated 1934. It was not until I began researching this book that I discovered the story of Raymond's war service.

The grave of Raymond J. Hickey at St. Stephen's Cemetery, Framingham. *Photo by author.*

Military enthusiasts enjoy touring the fields and forests across the globe where great battles took place. Standing in these spaces helps them imagine the chaos of the fight and the conflicting emotions of terror and courage of those fighting. One can get a similar experience in Massachusetts, standing on the deck of a battleship or destroyer built in Quincy or Boston, praying in a hospital chapel in Framingham or walking on the crumbling remains of a gun placement in Boston Harbor. The war on the homefront, on the other hand, was fought by ordinary people in ordinary places: the train stations, town greens, city halls and private homes of the state's 351 cities and towns. Those of us who happen to live in a house built before the war have the privilege of standing in kitchens where beleaguered moms created meals without the basic ingredients of milk, butter and meat; in backyards where Victory Gardens flourished; in garages where paper and rubber were stored before being hauled to the salvage drive; in living rooms and parlors where moms and dads read the daily newspaper and listened to news reports and presidential addresses on the radio. While I was working on this book in my Arthur Street home, the Hickey family was never far from my thoughts, as I pictured them struggling with the daily challenges of life during wartime, from the mildly inconvenient to the devastatingly tragic. The fact that a young man barely out of his teens left this house to serve his country and never returned is a powerful reminder to me of the sacrifice made by him and thousands like him. I am honored to share his story and add it to the annals of American heroes.

Chapter 6

EXPLORATION

Most of the military sites mentioned in this book have been abandoned or repurposed over the last eight decades, but some reminders of these bustling centers of activity can still be found. What follows are descriptions of some of the sites that have been preserved in one way or another, allowing visitors to get a sense, however limited, of homefront living in Massachusetts. I have also included museums and historic sites devoted to telling the World War II story. Local historical societies contain an abundance of artifacts, photographs and documents that highlight the experience of each individual town.

AMERICAN HERITAGE MUSEUM
568 Main Street, Hudson, MA 01749
www.americanheritagemuseum.org
Operated by the Collings Foundation, this museum houses one of the world's largest collections of military tanks, armored vehicles and aircraft, almost all of which are still operational. Although the museum's collection encompasses artifacts and vehicles from the Revolutionary War through the War on Terror, much of the collection is from the World War II era. Special events throughout the year include tank demonstrations, battle recreations featuring hundreds of reenactors and tank riding or driving experiences, which are available throughout the year.

Former ammunition bunker at the Assabet River National Wildlife Refuge. *Photo by author.*

Assabet River National Wildlife Refuge
(Maynard Ammunition Depot)
680 Hudson Road, Sudbury, MA 01776
www.fws.gov

The "Ammo Dump," as it was known, remained in army control under various names until it was transferred to the Fish and Wildlife Service in 2000. Today, it is known as the Assabet River National Wildlife Refuge. Covering over two thousand acres with miles of trails, this peaceful naturescape has a visitor's center and displays of the property's history. Most of the original fifty-five concrete ammunition bunkers are still located along the fifteen miles of trails.

Bare Cove Park (Hingham Naval Ammunition Depot)
Fort Hill Street, Hingham, MA 02043
www.hingham-ma.gov

Wompatuck State Park (Hingham Ammunition Depot Annex)
204 Union Street, Hingham, MA 02043
www.mass.gov
In 1972, the Town of Hingham acquired about 485 acres of the former depot site for the creation of Bare Cove Park. Several of the former munitions buildings survive and are used by local organizations, but most of the park consists of walking trails and a wildlife sanctuary. The park also contains a memorial dedicated to seventeen sailors from the Ammunition Depot who were killed in the explosion and sinking of a navy barge on May 11, 1944. The freight lighter YSS *YF-415* left the ammunition depot carrying ten crew members and a work crew of mostly African Americans, who were tasked with disposing of 150 tons of obsolete ordnance, including black powder, bullets, rockets and shells. The crew was about fifteen miles offshore and had nearly finished dumping the ordnance overboard when a tremendous explosion erupted, and the barge became engulfed in flames. Although fourteen survivors were rescued by the navy ship USS *Zircon*, seventeen members of the disposal crew were killed, and only one man's body was recovered. The memorial stone was dedicated in 2012 and paid for by J.B. Mills, a navy veteran who had been stationed at the depot with the sailors who died in the tragedy.

The former annex site today is the 3,500-acre Wompatuck State Park, located in the towns of Hingham, Scituate, Cohasset and Norwell. The park contains forty miles of trails and a 250-site campground. Several war-era concrete bunkers can be seen along the trails, but most have been demolished.

Battleship Cove
5 Water Street, Fall River, MA 02721
www.battleshipcove.org
Battleship Cove is both a war memorial and a historic military museum located in Fall River. Its featured attraction is the battleship USS *Massachusetts*, which was built at the Fore River Shipyard in 1941. Other ships housed at the site are the World War II–era submarine USS *Lionfish*, destroyer USS *Joseph P. Kennedy Jr.*, PT boats *617* and *796* and LCM *56*, a Higgins boat, which is the type of landing craft used on the beaches of Normandy in the D-day invasion. A trip to this unique museum will give you access to these ships and allow you to see up close what shipboard life was like during the war. Battleship Cove is also home to the official memorials for the State of Massachusetts to those lost in World War II, Korea, Vietnam, the Persian Gulf War and 9/11.

Battleship Cove, Fall River. *Photo by author.*

A view from the deck of the USS *Massachusetts*. *Photo by author.*

BOSTON HARBOR ISLANDS

The thirty-four harbor islands are part of both the national park and the state park system, and several of the islands with a World War II history are accessible by ferry. Fort Warren on George's Island is more strongly associated with the Civil War but still contains some remnants of its twentieth-century use. Paddock's Island was the site of Fort Andrew, where Italian POWs were held. A number of structures remain but are closed to the public for safety reasons. Several former gun batteries and the remains of Fort Standish can be found on Lovell's Island.

CHARLESTOWN NAVY YARD

www.nps.org

After the navy yard closed in 1974, 30 acres of the 130-acre site were designated as a national historic site. The Charlestown Navy Yard is part of the Boston National Historic Park System. While it may be best known as the home of the USS *Constitution* (Old Ironsides), it also houses a World

The USS *Cassin Young* at the Charlestown Navy Yard. *Photo by author.*

War II museum and the Fletcher-class destroyer USS *Cassin Young*. Although built in California in 1943, the *Cassin Young* is representative of many of the destroyers built at the navy yard during the war.

CUSHING MEMORIAL PARK (Cushing General Hospital)
60 Dudley Road, Framingham, MA 01702
www.framingham.gov

After serving as a veterans' hospital and geriatric center, the hospital property was sold to the Town of Framingham in 1999. A portion of the land was used to build a senior community while the remainder was kept as open space. The chapel was restored and is the only building that remains from its time as an army hospital. You can walk around the one-and-a-half-mile path and see mature trees that were originally planted by German POWs.

FENWAY VICTORY GARDENS
1200 Boylston Street, Boston, MA 02115
www.fenwayvictorygardens.org

First planted in 1942, the Fenway Victory Gardens are the only Victory Gardens still actively maintained in their original location. The seven-and-a-half-acre site contains over five hundred separate gardens maintained by members. Each year, the gardens host an open house, during which the public is invited to tour the grounds and meet the volunteers.

FORT DEVENS MUSEUM
94 Jackson Road, Devens, MA 01434
fortdevensmuseum.org

The Fort Devens Museum is a private nonprofit organization located in a former barracks on the property that was once Fort Devens. Its two large rooms feature exhibits and artifacts chronicling the fort's history from its inception in 1917 to the present day. While the museum does not have official army records for the thousands of men and women who came through the camp, it does have a wide range of documents, artifacts and photographs available to researchers. Located nearby is the post cemetery containing the graves of over nine hundred service members and family members dating back several hundred years. One section of the two-acre cemetery contains the graves of two Italian and twenty German POWs, including U-boat commander Friedrich Steinhoff. Also nearby is the only temporary camp building remaining from the World War II era. The former Red Cross building is well preserved and presently houses several businesses.

FORT REVERE PARK
60 Farina Road, Hull, MA 02045
www.mass.gov
Telegraph Hill in Hull was fortified as early as 1776 and was an important part of the defense of Boston Harbor through World War II. The park is maintained by the Metropolitan Park System of Greater Boston, and many of the fortifications are well preserved.

FORT TABER–FORT RODMAN MILITARY MUSEUM
1000C Rodney French Boulevard, New Bedford, MA 02744
www.forttaber.org
This museum is located within Fort Taber Park and is a treasure-trove of artifacts from the Revolution through the most recent American conflicts. The World War II section features photos, weapons, war diaries, battle souvenirs, models and a variety of other items from the war years. A walk around the grounds of this city-owned park will take you past the Civil War–era fort and remains of several gun placements.

MYLES STANDISH INDUSTRIAL PARK (Camp Myles Standish)
Industrial Park Road, Taunton, MA 02780
The camp closed after the war ended and for many years was home to the Paul A. Dever State School. Now an industrial park, there is a small area just inside the entrance with a memorial plaque and an information board. Tucked in the back is a stone grotto devoted to the Virgin Mary, built by Italian prisoners in 1943.

PATTON HOMESTEAD
650 Asbury Street, South Hamilton, MA 01982
www.pattonhomestead.org
Home to the Patton family for seventy years, the property is owned and operated by the Town of Hamilton and used for cultural, educational and

The grotto at Myles Standish Industrial Park, Taunton. *Photo by author.*

educational opportunities. It also houses the Patton archives, which are managed by the Wenham Museum. Nearby is Payton Park, a recreational area that contains a Sherman tank that saw action with Patton's Third Army.

SOUTH WEYMOUTH NAVAL AIR STATION

A portion of the former navy property has been developed as condos and single-family homes, but much of it remains undeveloped, with traces of old landing strips still visible. Shea Memorial Park features several informational installations and memorial plaques, as well as an A-4 Skyhawk jet mounted on a pedestal. It is located off Route 18 near the old main entrance.

SPRINGFIELD ARMORY NATIONAL HISTORIC SITE

One Armory Square, Suite 2, Springfield, MA 01105

www.nps.org

The Springfield Armory maintains and operates historic buildings and landscaping on fifty-five acres through the combined efforts of the National Park Service, the Commonwealth of Massachusetts, Springfield Technical Community College and the City of Springfield. The Main Arsenal building houses a visitor's center and museum. The Armory Museum boasts the world's largest collection of American military firearms, including multiple examples of the famed World War II service rifle, the M-1.

UNITED STATES NAVAL SHIPBUILDING MUSEUM/USS SALEM

(Fore River Shipyard)

739 Washington Street, Quincy, MA 02169

www.uss-salem.org

The former shipyard is now home to the United States Naval Shipbuilding Museum, which is housed within the heavy cruiser USS *Salem*, built at the shipyard in 1945. Visitors are welcome to tour several decks of the ship and view displays of model ships, photographs and other artifacts that highlight some of the hundreds of ships built at the historic shipyard.

A memorial to two Royal Air Force pilots flying out of Squantum who crashed on the Needham/Wellesley line on D-day, 1944. *Photo by author.*

MEMORIALS

There are six memorials in the state honoring the service members who perished in plane crashes during the war. The memorials are in Haverhill, Needham, North Reading, Peru, South Hadley and Uxbridge.

THREE CHAPELS

Each of the military bases in Massachusetts had a multidenominational chapel (Camp Edwards had thirteen!). Religious services as well as entertainment such as movies and stage shows were held here at each camp. After the war, several of these chapels were repurposed and survive to this day some eighty years after their construction.

Two of the chapels were disassembled and relocated to serve as Catholic churches. In 1946, the chapel at Camp Framingham was rebuilt in Marshfield to serve the parish of St. Ann by the Sea, which had lost its original church

The army chapel at Camp Framingham. *Courtesy of the Framingham History Center.*

The same chapel after it was relocated to Marshfield. *Author's collection.*

This chapel was moved from Camp Myles Standish to serve as St. Elizabeth Church in Milton for seventeen years. *Author's collection.*

The chapel at Cushing Park, Framingham. *Photo by author.*

building in the great fire of 1941. That building is still in use today as the parish center.

Also in 1946, the Archdiocese of Boston created the new parish of St. Elizabeth in Milton to serve the overcrowded parishes in Dorchester. Father Joseph Keenan, new pastor and a former navy lieutenant commander and chaplain, arranged for an army surplus chapel to be transported from Camp Myles Standish and rebuilt on Reedsdale Road. The chapel was opened on March 22, 1947, by Archbishop Richard Cushing and dedicated to Milton's war dead. The old chapel stood for another seventeen years until a permanent stone church was built and dedicated on Easter Sunday in 1964.

The brick chapel at Cushing Park in Framingham is the only building left of the original army hospital. At the time it was built, the pews and stained-glass windows were paid for by local organizations. The chapel was restored in 1999. It is owned by the City of Framingham and can be rented for private ceremonies such as weddings, funerals, baptisms and memorial services.

TIMELINE

1940

April 6: Groundbreaking ceremonies at Westover Field

April: Hitler and Germany invade Belgium and Netherlands

June: France falls to German army

September: FDR announces destroyers to Britain

September: London Blitz

September 16: First peacetime draft since Civil War requires all males ages twenty-one to forty-five register for mandatory one-year service

September: Camp Edwards on Cape Cod is leased to army and expanded

October 30: FDR gives campaign speech at Boston Garden

November: FDR wins unprecedented third term as president

1941

March: Lend-Lease program begins

May: Office of Civilian Defense established

May 1: Defense Bond program announced (renamed the War Bond Program after Pearl Harbor attack)

June 22: Hitler invades Russia

July: Nationwide aluminum drive

August 2: Silk production in United States is halted

August 3: Nighttime gas sales (7:00 p.m.–7:00 a.m.) banned

August 3: FDR fishes off Cape Cod, meets secretly with Churchill off Newfoundland and signs the Atlantic Charter

August 12: Senate votes to extend service of draftees an additional eighteen months

August 21: Office of Price Administration established

September 23: The battleship USS *Massachusetts* is launched at Quincy shipyard

October: Work begins on the Hingham Ammunition Annex

December 7: Pearl Harbor is attacked

December 8: United States declares war on Japan

December 8: Great Britain declares war on Japan

December 8: Civil Air Patrol recruiting begins

December 9: A false alarm sends residents of Greater Boston into a panic

December 9: President Roosevelt declares enemy alien status for Japanese, Germans and Italians

December 11: Germany and Italy declare war on United States

1942

January: War Production Board established

January: Dogs for Defense Program introduced

January 1: Automobile production ends

January 5: Rubber tire rationing begins

January 9: Governor Saltonstall announces the "Victory through Salvage" campaign

January: Red Sox catcher and coach Moe Berg retires from baseball to become goodwill ambassador

February: The United States goes on Daylight Savings Time (Eastern War Time) for the duration

February 9: Registration begins for all "enemy aliens" over the age of fourteen

March 1: The South Weymouth Naval Air Station is dedicated

March 8: Government seizes four square miles of land for ammo dump in Maynard, Stow, Hudson and Sudbury

April: Women Accepted for Volunteer Emergency Service (WAVES) established

May 1: The Hollywood Caravan comes to Boston

May 4–8: Sugar rationing begins
May 22: Red Sox left fielder Ted Williams enlists in the U.S. Navy
June 15–30: National Scrap Rubber Drive
July 22: Gas rationing begins on East Coast
September 27: Ted Williams plays his last game for the Red Sox for three years in a 7–6 win over the first-place Yankees
September 30: Men's rubber boots and work shoes rationed
August 31: Natick holds a war bond rally and buries an effigy of Hitler in a midnight ceremony
October: Eighteen-year-olds allowed to enlist
October 8: Camp Myles Standish opens
October 19: All restrictions on Italian citizens are lifted
November 29: Coffee is rationed
November 30: First War Bond Drive begins
November 30: New England dimout regulations take effect
December 1: Nationwide "Victory" speed limit of thirty-five miles per hour established
December 8: The Boston health commissioner announces regulations for sale of horse meat in the city

1943

February 9: Leather shoe rationing begins
March 1: New point system for rationing introduced. Among the over three hundred foods added to the rationing list are butter and canned, dried and frozen fruits and vegetables. The list is expanded at the end of the month to include meats.
April 6: DuPont Lucite manufacturing opens in Leominster
May 24: Ban on pleasure driving
June: The Japanese "suicide sub" comes to Boston on its nationwide tour
July 28: Coffee rationing ends
September 6: British prime minister Winston Churchill arrives in Cambridge under heavy guard and secrecy to accept an honorary degree at Harvard University
September 8: Citizens across the state celebrate the surrender of Italy
September 10: Hollywood War Bond Cavalcade
November 1: The eighteen-month dimout of New England states ends

1944

January: Cushing General Hospital opens in Framingham

February: First German POWs arrive at Fort Devens

February 1: Senator Henry Cabot Lodge Jr. resigns his Senate seat to return to active duty in the army

April 13: Tech Sergeant Raymond J. Hickey of Framingham is shot down over Germany

May 29: Aircraft observation posts closed across the state due to the enemy's "lowered strategic ability to carry any large-scale bombing attack to this country"

June 6: D-day invasion

June 6: Two British flyers killed in a plane crash in Needham

June 13: The Boston-based fishing trawler *Lark* attacked by U-boat U-*171*

June: First German POWs arrive at Camp Edwards on Cape Cod

June 15: 160,000 paper bombs are dropped on Boston and vicinity

August: The government announces milkweed pod collection in twenty-seven states

August: Governor Leverett Saltonstall's son Peter is killed in action in Guam

September 27: Former senator Henry Cabot Lodge Jr. captures four German soldiers in Italy

November 4: FDR rally at Fenway Park

November 7: FDR is elected president for a fourth term

November 7: Republican governor Leverett Saltonstall wins a special election to finish the Senate term of Henry Cabot Lodge Jr.

November 7: Boston Democratic mayor Maurice Tobin is elected governor

November 14: George Burns and Gracie Allen perform their radio show live from Symphony Hall, headline a fundraiser at Boston Garden the following day

1945

March: The USS *Franklin* is struck by two bombs dropped from a plane off the coast of Japan; Father Joseph O'Callahan is a hero

April 12: President Roosevelt dies at Warm Springs, Georgia; Harry S. Truman becomes the thirty-third president

May 5: Germany surrenders

May 8: V-E Day is celebrated

May: Fifty-four crew members of the German U-boat U-*873* are transported by bus to Boston after surrendering their vessel in Portsmouth, New Hampshire. Three days later, Commander Fritz Steinmach commits suicide in the Charles Street Jail

June 9: General George S. Patton gives a speech at the Hatch Shell in Boston after greeting a million well-wishers along his route from Bedford

August 6: Atomic bomb dropped on Hiroshima

August 9: Atomic bomb dropped on Nagasaki

August 14: Japan surrenders

August 15: "Little Mister Victory" baby is abandoned on Boston Common

August 22: The DuPont Lucite plant in Leominster closes

September 2: World War II officially ends

September 6: USS *Frankovich*, last ship built at Hingham Shipyard, is commissioned

December 21: General George S. Patton Jr. dies in Germany

1946

December 3: James Kilroy of Halifax takes delivery of a forty-foot streetcar, a prize for the most convincing story that he is the mysterious "Kilroy"

1947

October 19: The first war dead arrive in New York from Europe

BIBLIOGRAPHY

Bailey, Ronald H. *The Home Front: USA*. New York: Time-Life Books, Inc., 1978.

Boyer, Sarah. *Common Cause, Uncommon Courage: World War II and the Home Front in Cambridge, Massachusetts*. Cambridge, MA: Cambridge Historical Commission, 2009.

Butler, Gerald. *The Military History of Boston's Harbor Islands*. Charleston, SC: Arcadia Publishing, 2000.

———. *The Military History of the Cape Cod Canal*. Charleston, SC: Arcadia Publishing, 2002.

Cann, Donald, and John J. Galluzzo. *Camp Edwards and Otis Air Force Base*. Charleston, SC: Arcadia Publishing, 2010.

———. *Squantum and South Weymouth Naval Air Station*. Charleston, SC: Arcadia Publishing, 2004.

CBI Roundup. "Army-Trained Canines Flush Japs in Burma." 2, no. 52 (September 7, 1944).

City of Haverhill. *Haverhill in World War 2*. N.p., 1946.

Coffin, Leslie L. *Lew Ayres, Hollywood's Conscientious Objector*. Jackson: University Press of Mississippi, 2012.

Dallek, Matthew. *Defenseless Under the Night: The Roosevelt Years and the Origins of Homeland Security*. New York: Oxford University Press, 2016.

Davidoff, Nicholas. *The Catcher Was a Spy: The Mysterious Life of Moe Berg*. New York: Random House, 1994.

Doherty, Richard P. *History of the Massachusetts Committee on Public Safety 1940–1945*. Commonwealth of Massachusetts, 1945.

Earls, Alan R. *Watertown Arsenal*. Charleston, SC: Arcadia Publishing, 2007.

Gay, James A. *Battleship Cove*. Charleston, SC: Arcadia Publishing, 2014.

Goodwin, Doris Kearns. *No Ordinary Time: Franklin and Eleanor Roosevelt: The Home Front in World War II*. New York: Simon & Schuster, 1994.

Hannah, William. "Friends and Enemies: Co-Belligerents and Prisoners of War at Camp Myles Standish, Taunton, Massachusetts during World War II." *Bridgewater Review* 33, no. 2 (November 2014).

Kimble, James J. *Mobilizing the Home Front: War Bonds and Domestic Propaganda*. College Station: Texas A&M University Press, 2006.

Lingeman, Richard. *Don't You Know There's a War On? The American Home Front 1941–1945*. New York: G.P. Putnam, 1970.

McDonald, Christopher. *The Military History of New Bedford*. Charleston, SC: Arcadia Publishing, 2001.

Mehlo, Noel F. *D-Day General: How Dutch Cota Saved Omaha Beach on June 6, 1944*. Guilford, CT: Stackpole Books, 2021.

Needham Historical Society. *Needham*. Charleston, SC: Arcadia Publishing, 1997.

Nichter, Luke A. *The Last Brahmin: Henry Cabot Lodge, Jr., and the Making of the Cold War*. New Haven, CT: Yale University Press, 2020.

Nowlan, Bill. *Ted Williams at War*. Burlington, MA: Rounder Books, 2007.

Piggott, Marc, ed. *The Defender's History: A Historical Account of Naval Air Station, South Weymouth, Mass*. Weymouth, MA: NAS South Weymouth Publisher, 1996.

Russell, Harold. *The Best Years of My Life*. Middlebury, VT: Paul S. Eriksson, Publisher, 1981.

Saltonstall, Leverett. *Salty: Recollections of a Yankee in Politics*. Boston: Boston Globe, 1976.

Schorow, Stephanie. *East of Boston: Notes from the Harbor Islands*. Charleston, SC: The History Press, 2008.

United States Army Air Forces. *Identification of Aircraft for Army Air Forces Ground Observer Corps*. Washington, D.C.: United States Government Printing Office, 1942.

United States Office of Civilian Defense. *What Can I Do: The Citizen's Handbook for War*. Washington, D.C., 1942.

Wallace, Frederick A. *Pushing for Cushing*. Framingham, MA: Damianos Publishing, 2016.

Wiberg, Eric. *U-Boats in New England*. Charleston, SC: Fonthill Media, 2019.

INDEX

Q

Quincy, MA 12, 19, 28, 30, 70, 85, 92, 94, 95, 115, 124, 130

R

Roosevelt, Eleanor 12, 32
Roosevelt, President Franklin 11, 13, 18, 25, 65, 83, 91, 104, 106, 113, 129, 130, 132, 133
Russell, Harold 74, 75

S

Saltonstall, Leverett 13, 21, 22, 39, 45, 46, 55, 67, 69, 79, 130, 132
Somerville, MA 62, 76, 112
South Weymouth Naval Air Station 85, 87, 94, 124, 130
Springfield Armory 26, 96, 124
Springfield, MA 28, 62, 113
Stimson, Henry 13, 83

T

Tobin, Maurice 28, 47, 50, 55, 68, 108, 110, 132
Truman, President Harry S. 107, 109, 133

U

USS *Franklin* 76, 133
USS *Potomac* 18

V

Victory Gardens 49, 50, 121

W

Walsh, David I. 11, 68
war bonds 14, 35, 41, 44, 57, 58
Watertown Arsenal 96
Westover Air Base 12, 97, 129
Williams, Ted 15, 69, 70, 112, 131

ABOUT THE AUTHOR

James L. Parr taught elementary school for thirty-four years before retiring in June 2022. He is a longtime volunteer at several local historical organizations and community theater groups. This is Jim's fourth book for The History Press; other titles include *Framingham Legends and Lore*, *Murder and Mayhem in Metrowest Boston* (both with Kevin A. Swope) and *Dedham: Historic and Heroic Tales of Shiretown*.